JUST WAR

Pat

HEBREWS 1:14

JUST WAR
A SOLDIER'S REVELATION

TOM NEWMAN

TATE PUBLISHING
AND ENTERPRISES, LLC

Published by Tate Publishing & Enterprises, LLC
127 E. Trade Center Terrace | Mustang, Oklahoma 73064 USA
1.888.361.9473 | www.tatepublishing.com

Tate Publishing is committed to excellence in the publishing industry. The company reflects the philosophy established by the founders, based on Psalm 68:11,
"The Lord gave the word and great was the company of those who published it."

Book design copyright © 2013 by Tate Publishing, LLC. All rights reserved.
Cover design by Gordon Maronde
Interior design by Caypeeline Casas

Published in the United States of America

ISBN: 978-1-62854-991-1
1. Biography & Autobiography / Personal Memoirs
2. History / Military / Vietnam War
13.08.29

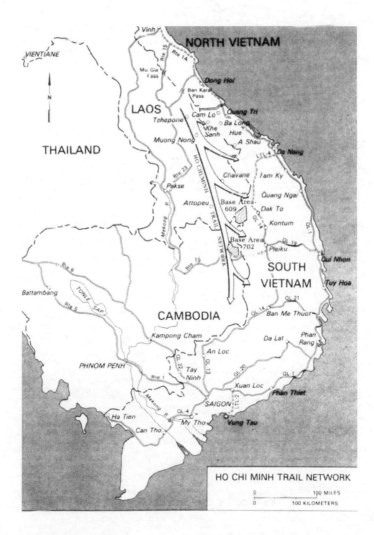

HO CHI MINH TRAIL NETWORK

0   100 MILES

0   100 KILOMETERS

DEDICATION

Laika, my friend.

By this we have come to know love: that he laid down his life on our behalf. And we are obligated to lay down our lives for the brothers.

1 John 3:16 (NASB)

Ariel, my daughter.
Deitric, my son.

I have no greater joy than this: to hear that my children are walking in the truth.

3 John 1:4 (NASB)

ACKNOWLEDGMENTS

I would like to acknowledge the Trinity and His constant and continual involvement in the lives, events, and relationships of those who put their trust in Christ. And to the ministering spirits sent to minister to all that are about to inherit salvation. (Heb 1:14 NASB)

I am very much appreciative of my children, Ariel and Deitric for their input, feedback, encouragement, time, involvement and continual support in this project. It was after all their idea to put these experiences to print. I am also indebted to Deitric in his creativity in providing the title of the book.

I am blessed to have as a friend, Gordon Maronde, a very gifted and talented artist who produced the cover for the book and provided the tagline; *A Soldier's Revelation. @ nationalfineart.com*

Alexis Selzler at Tate Publications for her expertise and insights in insuring the final product is fluent and easily readable by all audiences.

I am also grateful that Tate Publishing has a position of accepting and contracting with unpublished authors to help them break into the world of sharing thoughts, experiences and ideas.

I would also like to acknowledge the encouragement and insights provided by; Michelle Livingston, John Woodcock, Jim Nelson, Mike and Krista Newman.

There are many that cannot be acknowledged, and a few that can be from among the ranks of the paratroopers of the O-Deuce, with the 101st Airborne Division in Vietnam in 1968. Their names are within.

TABLE OF CONTENTS

FOREWORD

Dear Deitric,

You asked me to write a letter to you explaining my experiences in Vietnam. You had heard me talk about the war. I was never reluctant to answer questions you and Ariel had. You said you wanted the letter so that you could better understand the person I am, by understanding the experiences I went through. You asked me to be completely honest and tell you what I thought, felt and exactly what I had experienced, and not to pull any punches.

When I returned from my tour of duty, I had a lot of questions about life, death, faith, God, eternity, and other dimensions. I enrolled in the University of Minnesota, but that is a secular environment so the information was not much help for the questions I had. I tried to put it all behind me. I got involved in a career and married your mother.

Then Ariel and you were born. The miracle of birth brought all of the questions back to the forefront. When Ariel was born, I was awestruck by the miracle and just plain fascinated at the thought of a child, a new human life that was a part of me. Then when you were born, I thought, *Okay, there is more to this than just another life to love and care for.* I felt an incredible responsibility for you two. I was responsible for the souls of two people. Along with that responsibility, came the knowledge that I had better do a lot of things very right. I have always been a man of faith; however, there now seemed to be an urgency for me to understand as much as I could so that I would do the right things for you two.

The year you were born, I thought Scripture says "Children are a gift from God" (Psalm 127:3, NASB), so Scripture is where I better get my instructions. I began getting up at 5:00 a.m. so that I could spend an hour in Scripture every morning before I began my normal routine. I remember telling you, kids, I am fallible and I am going to make mistakes, so if I tell you to do or to not do something, it's not because I say so, it's because it's from Scripture—God says so. I continued to get up at five every morning to read Scripture. When you were eleven, you began getting up at five with me so you could read Scripture, and you did so until you were thirteen. When you joined me that first morning, I asked you if you were going to read scripture with me, you replied, "This must be pretty important if you get up at 5:00 every morning to read, so I better find out what it is all about." I continue daily reading of Scripture to this day, as do you.

As I read Scripture, I also began to find the answers to all the questions that had been lingering with me since my tour of duty in Vietnam. I eventually found all of the answers to the questions I had.

When I told you and your sister that I had found all of the answers to the questions I had, you guys said there may be others looking for the same answers, put the answers in a book. The end result was the publication of *A Brief History of the Bible. The Essentials of Christianity within the Context of Our Physical and Spiritual Realities*.

When Dad and Sally died, and then Nancy, the letters I had written them from Vietnam were returned to me. They had kept every one of them. *Just War* is a product of the letter you asked me to write, which turned out to be twenty-five pages, augmented with the letters that were returned to me from my family.

Our culture always tries to rewrite history to match the current philosophies or to skew the direction of our culture in ways that justify current beliefs. When you change our history, you change who we are. *Just War* is an actual, truthful, and factual legacy of the Vietnam War in 1968 from the perspective of one infantry paratrooper.

INTRODUCTION

I think there is a lot of misunderstanding about the war in Vietnam. Unfortunately, our news media, for the most part, has given up on the original intent of reporting news, which is just that—reporting the news. Today, news outlets offer opinions more than they report the news. It seems like that about the time of the Vietnam era, the news media transformed from reporting the news to an agency that realized their power to sway public opinion. Since that time, the media has been the vehicle for shaping the American psyche. This has been much to the derogation of what it means to be an American citizen and the necessity of morality and religion to maintain our sovereignty as a nation.

This is an honest, unvarnished account of one paratrooper from the 101st Airborne Division in the I Corps of Vietnam in 1968—the bloodiest year of the war. I was with Bravo Company of the first of the 502nd or the O-Deuce. In the year I was with the O-Deuce, we sustained 97 percent casualties and fatalities. There were twenty-six times, that I know of, that I should have been killed or at least severely wounded. There was

also one time when I actually did die and was resuscitated, of course.

There are two terms you need to be familiar with:
foundational reality and *provisional* reality. I use
these terms to explain different dimensions of reality. Provisional reality is the touch and feel, the three
dimensional world we live in. Foundational reality
is the spiritual realm. It is not composed of any hard
matter it exists beyond the thin veil that separates the
two realities.

Let the truth be told.

ENLISTMENT

In the summer before my senior year of high school, I purchased a motorcycle because that was what I could afford for transportation. It was a very fast bike and that was how I rode it—fast. The natural consequence of that was the accumulation of a number of speeding tickets. When I appeared before the judge for my seventh speeding ticket, he was going to revoke my driver's license until I was twenty-one. This was not a very promising prospect.

My father had told us kids that he could not afford to send all five of us to college, so he would not pay for anyone's college education. I had been working evenings, part time, in a factory that produced computer frames, and I knew that was not the type of work I wanted to do for the rest of my life. If the judge suspended my driving privileges, I would be on foot, which certainly would limit my employment opportunities as we were living in the suburbs.

I had thought about the military as a career option, but I never thought too hard about it. All I knew about the military was the Hollywood's pre-1970 versions—

long on glory and short on reality. I told the judge that I was considering joining the military. He said, if I did that and showed him my enlistment papers, he would forego suspending my license.

There were other factors that also weighed into my decision-making process. I have always had a lot of national pride. I was a product of the JFK generation, "Ask not what your country can do for you, ask what you can do for your country." I have always been fiercely independent, as most Americans are, and was always deeply concerned about the oppression of people by their governments or other countries inflicting their will on those less able to defend themselves.

I made the decision to enlist in the Army in June of 1967. Thirty days after my graduation, I reported to Fort Campbell, Kentucky.

When I enlisted, I was asked what I wanted to do in the Army. My thoughts were that we were at war, trying to help an oppressed people from being subjugated to a power not of their choosing. I volunteered for the infantry and jump school so I could be a paratrooper. I also volunteered for duty in Vietnam.

Now, this is a perspective from provisional reality. Spiritual acuity would tell me that from God's perspective in foundational reality, He was probably not very pleased with my pride, arrogance, and self-serving lifestyle. He probably was also not very pleased with the path I was on and the choices I was making. On my current path of self-will, I would not be able to accomplish God's will for my life. Because of my independence and self-sufficiency, He knew it would take more than a few trials and tribulations to get me on His path. So He sent me to war; however, He did not send me alone. He sent His *ministering spirits* to protect me and keep me safe. In all of life, these two truths are certain: First and foremost, God is sovereign over His creation; therefore, when we are called, we have no choice but to respond. Second, if you are one of God's children, everything that happens in your life is either orchestrated by or permitted by God.

This whole business of going to war is all about concepts that are intangible—liberty, freedom, a life free of oppression. Ideas that have their value in what people are willing to pay to assure their preservation. People can say that freedom and liberty are important to them; but if those values are threatened and they acquiesce to the threat, the concepts do not have much meaning. On the other hand, if someone or some government says they are going to take your freedom, and you fight, or die trying, to preserve your freedom, that gives these values meaning. It is like anything else, it is worth whatever you are willing to pay for it that sets its value.

Any guy can talk a good story. It is a man's behavior in those real life situations that shows what he truly believes, and what he truly believes defines who he is.

INFANTRY TRAINING

In July of 1967, I reported for Basic Training at Fort Campbell, Kentucky, the home of the 101st Airborne Division. When a person first enters the military they are subject to a battery of testing. The tests are conducted so the military can get to know as much about the new recruits as possible. When I finished my testing, I was told that my scores were so high I could either become a helicopter pilot or go immediately into OCS (officer candidate school). OCS is a six month course, and upon completion, graduates are given the rank of second lieutenant. Almost all candidates entering OCS were college graduates. I told the officer in charge that I was eighteen years old, and I did not think six months of training would qualify me to be responsible for the lives of fifty men. I opted for flight school, only to find out that the army will not allow a left-handed person to fly helicopters. It is a right-handed world, and lefties tend to do a lot of things backwards. All of the gauges and controls are designed for right-handers. There is also the phenomenon that only left-handers understand, that is that most things are backwards. Our tendency is to turn things and orientate ourselves in the opposite direction. The whole idea behind *Alice in Wonderland* was to demonstrate what it is like for a left-hander to live in a right-handed world. Have you ever seen a left-hander back up a boat trailer at a boat landing? They are the guys that almost miss the apron and have to make repeated attempts to back up in order to align their trailer with the ramp.

Basic Training is two months of training with a few objectives. Primarily, to teach the average American how to become a soldier. Secondly, the training is very rigorous and is designed to put a new recruit in the best physical shape they have ever been in. Thirdly, rigors of training also tend to wash out those that will not be able to withstand the extreme demands of combat. I also learned that I was an excellent marksman. Currently in the United States only 27 percent of young adults between the ages of seventeen and twenty-four qualify for service in the armed forces.

When I graduated from Basic Training, I went to AIT (Advance Infantry Training). AIT is much more rigorous with training, considerably more sophisticated than Basics. AIT is also a two-month training curriculum. In AIT, we learned how to read maps, how to call in artillery fire, air strikes, field first aid, hand-to-hand combat, bayonet skills, jungle survival, field maneuvers, how to use the PRC radio, ambush techniques, counter insurgence, jungle fighting, city-street fighting, and a host of combat techniques.

A major focus of the training was on the effective use of small arms. We gained proficiencies with the

M16, M14, .45 calaber semiautomatic handgun, M60 machine gun and the M79 grenade launcher. The M16 is a fully automatic rifle with a selection for semiautomatic. It has a maximum effective range of 460 meters and a rate of fire of 20 rounds in 1.2 seconds. The M14 was a semiautomatic rifle in 7.62 mm or .308 caliber; it had an effective range of 1,200 meters. I would later use a Match M14 in sniper school. Match rifles and ammunition are specifically designed for accuracy.

We also gained experience with chemical warfare defense, hand grenades, claymore mines, and the LAW, which is an acronym for Light Anti-tank Weapon. The LAW is a portable weapon that fires a 66mm projectile and is accurate up to 300 meters, although it had a range of 1,000 meters. It was designed to disable armored vehicles.

A typical day started at four thirty with a three-mile run, an hour of calisthenics, and then breakfast. Once a soldier was airborne qualified, a paratrooper, they were required to run five miles every morning. We spent a lot of time at the rifle range in classes and shooting. Sometimes, we would go the range by truck, if they were available, otherwise we would march or double time. There were several firing ranges and they were anywhere from twelve to twenty-two miles from the barracks. We would have a few hours of instruction then spend the day on the range becoming proficient with small arms. The military is short on theory and long on practical application.

Often, we would be told that we would have rides back to the barracks, only to be told the trucks were not coming. This happened so often that we suspected the drill instructors wanted us to get use to disappointments and things not always turning out as anticipated.

The drill sergeant for our platoon was Sgt. Thode. One day on our return from the range Sgt. Thode ordered me.

"Newman, fall out and call cadence."

I improvised a little and called cadence to the tune of the theme song for *The Mickey Mouse Clubhouse*.

"Left, right, left, right. Who's the leader of the club that's made for you and me?" I continued…"S-g-t, s-g-t, t-h-o-d-e!"

"Sgt. Thode, Sgt. Thode."

"Newman! Platoon, drop and give me fifty! I want you to push Kentucky away from Tennessee."

Sgt. Thode failed to see the humor in that cadence.

After AIT, I reported to Fort Benning, Georgia, for Jump School. Three weeks and five jumps later, I was a paratrooper. The first jump is very hard to describe, a lot of noise from the engines, the noise of the wind rushing in the door, and the fear and apprehension of jumping. After jumping out of the plane, the next thing I realized is that everything was just peace and quiet. I could see off into the distance for miles into the horizon, and I was just gently descending towards the earth. Amazing!

There was another left-handed issue here during landing. When a trooper gets close to the ground they *pull a slip*, which means to pull the cords on one side of the chute to dump out the air. This slows your descent just before you land and execute a PLF (parachute landing fall). Lefties tended to pull their slip on the wrong side of the chute. Instead of dumping the air out of the chute, it acted more like a sail. Lefties didn't do PLFs until they got the hang of it. Their landings were called "crash and burn."

Certainly, the most interesting training exercise we ever had was at the end of Jump School. We were loaded into airplanes at Fort Benning Georgia and dropped into the everglades in Florida. We were dropped in small groups, given a map, a compass, and some provisions. We were told we would have, it was either a day or two, to find the rendezvous point for a ride back to Fort Benning. We were also told if we missed the rendezvous we would have to walk back. Of Course we landed in the swamps, knee to waist deep in water. The insects, snakes and other things in the everglades were probably good training, but none of us were too excited about this training exercise. I'm not sure if we were really in the everglades because we never saw any alligators, but that is what they told us.

There were 1,100 men on the first day of training and a little over 500 at the graduation ceremony, another process of elimination. The philosophy behind Jump School is that any normal person looking at the ground from an airplane, anticipating jumping out of the plane will be, at least, apprehensive and the first time downright scared. The training imparts a trooper with the ability to do what they have to do no matter how scared they are.

I then applied for Ranger School, but I was told my orders had come in for Vietnam. The drill instructor told me not to worry though. If I came back, I would be more than qualified to be a ranger, and he would give me my ranger tab. Of course, he wasn't around when I returned from Vietnam, and I reported to a different post anyway. So I never received my ranger tab.

IN COUNTRY

February of 1968, seven months after I had enlisted in the Army, I arrived in Vietnam. 1968 would turn out to be the deadliest year of the war. I would spend my nineteenth year in Vietnam.

My original duty station was to be a bunker guard in Bien Hoa, which is in the southern portion of South Vietnam. It would have been a relatively safe assignment; defensive rather than offensive, and I would venture pretty boring. Somehow, at the airport, I was directed to the wrong plane and wound up in Phu Bai, which is in I Corps, the northern most part of South Vietnam.

The sergeant at the Phu Bai airport checked everyone's orders, when he looked at mine, he realized I was in the wrong place. The sergeant said the 101st was right in the middle of the Tet Offensive and was in dire need of replacements. He said he would just change my orders and assign me to the 502nd, or the O-Deuce. This also was God's plan. "All things"—no matter how bad they seem—"work to the good for those who love the Lord." (Romans 8:28 NASB)

I was sent with another trooper to LZ (Landing Zone) Sally. However, the Army Corps of Engineers hadn't started building the LZ yet, so we were routed back to An Lo Bridge. An Lo was an old French outpost built to defend the bridge. The 502nd, the heart of the 101st Airborne Division, was using An Lo Bridge as its operational headquarters. As the heart of the 101st, members of the O-Deuce had a red heart painted on each side of our helmets, just over the ear. I reported to the CO (commanding officer) for my assignment. While I was waiting to see the CO, a trooper showed me seven helmets with bullet holes right through the hearts painted on the helmets. I don't know if this was staged or not, but it had the intended effect: Always be on the alert for snipers.

When we first started using An Lo as a base of operation, there were a lot of VC (Vietcong) in the area. We would encounter sniper fire as we moved out and along our route. We also encountered booby traps, and an occasional ambush. By May, because of our presence and activities, the area around An Lo was fairly secure and the local population began to move back.

The French had taught the Vietnamese how to bake bread. We looked forward to having fresh baked baguettes on our return from a long stint in the field. I used to save the peanut butter and jelly from my rations. I would relish the idea of peanut butter and jelly sandwich on a freshly baked baguette.

When the locals began to repopulate the village, they would also set up shop. Their dwellings were called hooches. They were small, housed a single family and

were, basically a thatched hut made from dried vegetation, cardboard, and occasionally corrugated sheet
metal. The front of their hooch was like a garage door
and when it was time to conduct some business they
would lift up the front of the hooch. All that was really
for sale was rice, rice wine, Tiger beer, Coke, bananas,
bread fruit, and anything else they could obtain from
other GIs. They would also make things if you brought
in the material. I had a *mama-san* make a vest out of
the canvas from a shelter half. The vest held twenty
magazines for my M16. There was also a barber in An
Lo that would give haircuts to the troopers when we
were back on stand downs.

One evening, we set up an ambush for any VC that
were operating in the area. There were about six VC
that walked into our ambush. When we reviewed the
results of the ambush in the morning, among the dead
was the local barber. That was one of the biggest chal-
lenges we had; the VC lived with the local population.
They were citizen by day and soldiers or guerilla fighters at night.

The only disparaging activities committed by members of the O-Deuce were that two troopers on separate
occasions each raped a Vietnamese girl. They thought
it would be better to spend two years in Leavenworth
prison than to spend one year in Vietnam.

I CORPS

The 502nd was using the old French outpost, at An Lo, as their base of operations as we did not have a firebase yet. Firebases would be built at strategic points across Vietnam to provide a base for helicopter operations, artillery support, and a MASH (Mobile Army Surgical Hospital) unit to support infantry operations. Prior to the arrival of the 101st in the I Corps, most of the US Army troops were stationed in II and III Corps. The Marines were the only troops in I Corps.

As enemy infiltration and activity increased dramatically in the I Corps, General Westmorland sent the 2nd Brigade of the 101st Airborne Division to I Corps consisting of Alpha, Bravo, and Charlie Companies of the 502nd and, later, the 501st. Westmoreland also sent elements of the 1st Air Cavalry Division to I Corps with their compliment of helicopters.

Westmorland had the marines stationed at Da Nang, Khe Sanh, Phu Bai, and on the DMZ (demilitarized zone). These were vital areas and needed a continual US troop presence. Phu Bai was the main marine base in I Corps. Da Nang was an airbase for helicopters, transports and fighter aircraft. The marines defended the base. The marines on the DMZ were there to maintain the integrity of the demilitarized zone to prevent the NVA and supplies from crossing into South Vietnam. Khe Sanh was in the mountains—in the dense jungles of western Vietnam. Khe Sanh was located about fifteen miles south of the DMZ and about six miles from the border with Laos. Khe Sanh was a key-entry point for troops and supplies from the North using the Ho Chi Minh trail.

The Ho Chi Minh trail ran through Laos and Cambodia paralleling the western border of Vietnam and was the major supply route from the North to the South. Another key-entry point just further south was the A Shau Valley.

I was assigned to Bravo Company, second platoon of the 502nd. I received my first assignment as a grenadier with the M79 grenade launcher. A trooper may cycle through several positions until there is a good match between the trooper's skill set and the company's needs. The M79 launches a 40 mm projectile and is effective for about 300 meters. There are a number of different projectiles that can be fired from the M79, including explosive, anti-personnel, smoke, buckshot, and flechette. Flechette, which is French for *little arrow*, are miniature darts, about an inch long with a barbed nose and stabilizing fin on the back. There were about fifty of these little darts in each round.

SOME TERMS

For clarification: Charlie refers collectively to the Vietcong (VC), the Viet Minh, or the North Vietnamese Regular Army soldiers (NVA).

Vietcong and Viet Minh were different names for the same force; Viet Minh while fighting the French and then Vietcong when referred to in our involvement. Their name change was so that Ho Chi Minh could lie to the signing nations of the Geneva Convention and say that all the Viet Minh were out of South Vietnam (which was a condition of the accord).

Vietcong were the indigenousness guerilla fighters who lived in South Vietnam. Whenever they could, they would carry out attacks against US and ARVN forces, usually at night. These were the black pajama people. They would conduct ambushes, set booby traps, conduct reconnaissance, infiltrate US base camps, and work with NVA troops when they were in the vicinity. They were also responsible for assassinating political figures and conducting terrorist activities to intimidate the people of South Vietnam.

The NVA were uniformed communist soldiers from North Vietnam. They were highly professional and highly trained by both the Soviets and the Chinese Red Army.

Russia sent advisors to Vietnam; they manned the anti-aircraft batteries and flew MIG jets for North Vietnam. The Chinese also sent advisers as training cadre. The Chinese sent 327,000 officers, soldiers, and cadre to North Vietnam to support the war effort against the US. We would encounter Chinese soldiers in the field working with the NVA.

Vietnam was divided into four combat zones. I Corps was the north end of South Vietnam, the area from the DMZ, south along the coast of the South China Sea to Da Nang, west to the Laotian border, and back north to the DMZ. I Corps is also the location of Khe Sanh, Hue, and the A Shau Valley. II Corps was called the central highlands and is where Pleiku and Cam Ranh Bay are located. III Corps was where Saigon was located. IV Corps was the Mekong Delta region.

The 1/502nd of the 101st, the unit I was with, operated in the I Corps. Our AO or area of operation was from the DMZ, south along the coastline of the South China Sea to Hue, west to the A Shau Valley near the Laotian Border, and back north to Khe Sanh. Our bases of operation were LZ Sally, An Lo Bridge, and Bastogne. Bastogne was a firebase in the mountains (*in the mountains* is synonymous with being in the jungles). Bastogne was built by the 101st Airborne in 1968 along with LZ Sally. Bastogne was named after the heroic stance of the 101st Airborne in World War II.

ARVNs were the military forces of the South Vietnamese government, the Army of the Republic of Vietnam. PFs were the Popular Forces of South Vietnam and were akin to a national police force.

There was one major highway in Vietnam, highway number 1, and it ran from Hanoi in the North to Saigon in the South. In our AO, none of the local villages had any running water or sewer system; they used the rice patty, which is why we could not eat the rice; and they had no electricity. Contrary to what Hollywood would have you believe, there were no brothels, let alone hot tubs, in the villages we visited, or at An Lo.

All of us ground troops carried a rucksack that held our provisions for about three days and weighed about ninety pounds. We carried a three-day ration of food, sleeping blanket to keep the mosquitoes away, half of a tent or shelter half, rain poncho for the monsoons, medical supplies, and as much water as we wanted to carry (four quarts were recommended). I carried 8, along with 200 rounds of M16 ammunition. I carried 400 rounds, 2 grenades were also recommended I carried 6, extra socks, a flak jacket that no one carried, insect repellant that would melt plastic, water purification tablets, malaria pills, salt tablets, megavitamins, an entrenching tool for digging, flashlight, compass, personal effects, books, stationary, and toiletries etc. We also rotated carrying extra machine gun ammo, claymore mines, extra rounds for the grenade launcher, or a LAW. The rucksack was designed so that a trooper could easily slip out of it then all that remained was the web belt, which held water, ammunition, and grenades.

In the year I was with the O-Deuce, we sustained 97 percent casualties and fatalities. It's hard to imagine death on such a grand scale, especially when it is so personal. Camaraderie is an after the fact phenomena, it is built on trust and honesty. When a person does not know if they are living their last day, their conversation is open, honest, and (as we used to refer to it,) gut-level communication. When a trooper relates their inner most fears, thoughts, and emotions they are building strong and sincere relationships. When I would lose a comrade, I had lost a good friend. The death of so many people, continually, caused me to reexamine everything I knew and held to be true.

During World War II, the average time an infantry-man spent in actual combat was forty days; in Vietnam, it was two hundred days. This was primarily the result of a couple of very important differences. Helicopters provided vast superiority in mobility compared to other wars. Instead of marching to find the enemy, when the enemy was spotted or there was good intel-ligence, infantry soldiers in Vietnam were choppered to the fight. Additionally, Vietnam was confined to a relatively very small geographic area compared to the island hopping in the Pacific or the vast expanse of the European Theater that covered many countries. Critics said we did not know how to fight a guerilla war, we did not know how to fight a Revolutionary War, or a Civil War either. Wars are fluid and dynamic with continu-ally evolving strategies on both sides.

General Westmorland chose to fight a mobile war with extensive use of helicopters while waiting for the chance to have a set-piece battle with the enemy. Conventional war strategy would say fight for a piece of land and hold it. From the newly acquired real estate soldiers would establish their *front line.* The soldiers would then continue to advance causing the enemy to retreat.

First, taking and holding real estate in the jungles is ill advised. The stationary target will be under constant bombardment with little opportunity to engage and defeat an unseen enemy. The vegetation was so thick, it would be difficult to know where the attacks were coming from. The enemy would be able to get very close to your position—launch an attack and retreat into the dense cover. Also, we did not have enough manpower to conduct that type of a war strategy. The only *line* was the border between Vietnam, Laos, and Cambodia.

Second, the most significant obstacle we had to contend with was not being able to strike the enemy at their base camps, supply depots, and artillery emplacements because they were located in Laos and Cambodia. President Johnson decreed that Laos and Cambodia were neutral territory and, therefore, off limits to any US military activity. The NVA fought their battles from neutral territory. They would infiltrate the south to conduct raids on installations, troops, or villages and then retreat back across the border to neutral ground.

A tour in Vietnam was 365 days. Captains or company commanders spent ninety days in the field, lieutenants spent six months in the field, and infantry rifleman or noncommissioned officers (NCOs) spent their entire tour in the field. I thought this was a very poor strategy as most of the NCOs had more experience than the officers. Most of the second lieutenants were right out of OCS (all book learning and no experience). Most did not last long. We went through thirteen second lieutenants during my twelve month tour. However, there were a couple of very capable lieutenants. One very accomplished lieutenant was Lt Land; he was one of the few that survived his tour of duty in Vietnam.

Tet was a major holiday in Vietnam, signifying the beginning of a new year; it was a religious holiday as well. The North Vietnamese strategy for the Tet Offensive in January of 1968 was to deliver a major military defeat to the South Vietnamese and American forces. It was also assumed that with a tremendous show of force and their victories there would be a popular uprising of the South Vietnamese population to overthrow the government of South Vietnam. The popular uprising never occurred.

A HISTORICAL PERSPECTIVE

Recent history of Vietnam began in 1941 when Ho Chi Minh sought independence from the French and Japanese. The Japanese had invaded Vietnam during World War II, which, at the time, was a French colony. The US actually offered assistance to Ho Chi Minh during the last couple of years of World War II to help him unseat the Japanese, our common enemy, at the time. The Viet Minh also helped recover American pilots who were shot down by the Japanese. When the war ended, the Japanese withdrew from China and Vietnam. Ho Chi Minh now wanted to rid his country of the French and establish an independent communist government. South Vietnam, the oldest surviving democracy, wanted to maintain its democratic republic. The Geneva Convention established a demilitarized zone on the 17th parallel in Vietnam, not unlike the one established in Korea. The DMZ was to separate the communist government of the north from the free democratic republic in the south. Ho was also to remove all of his Viet Minh fighters from the South. He did not remove them, he just renamed them Vietcong and said all of the Viet Minh were out of South Vietnam.

At the close of hostilities from World War II, Stalin, in 1945, offered Ho assistance. Stalin promised Ho Chi Minh unlimited manpower and resources if he could subdue South Vietnam, Laos, and Cambodia (jointly referred to as French Indonesia) and bring them under the communist umbrella. China (who borders Vietnam on the north and not wanting a Russian state bordering their own) also offered Ho unlimited support. Russia and China were both vying to win the loyalty of Ho Chi Minh as each wanted Vietnam to be their satellite state.

In 1947, the US became increasingly concerned about the spread of communism when Mao Tse-tung's Chinese Communist forces won the Chinese civil war. President Truman announced his, "Truman Doctrine," which was a policy whereby the US would support any free people who were resisting attempts of subjugation by armed minorities or outside pressures. Mao's victory meant Ho's Viet Minh would now have another powerful ally. In January of 1950, Communist China and the Soviet Union officially recognize Ho's Democratic Republic of Vietnam. China began to send military advisors and modern weapons to help the Viet Minh in their battle against the French. In July of the same year, President Harry Truman sent $15 million in military aid to the French. By the time the French withdrew from Vietnam in 1954, American aid to France reached $1 billion for the war effort against North Vietnam.

In 1950, President Truman establishes the MAAG, (Military Assistance Advisory Group) in Saigon to aid the French. The US also signed a Mutual Defense Assistance Agreement with France, Vietnam, Cambodia, and Laos.

In 1953, with the end of hostilities in Korea, China significantly increased its aid to North Vietnam. Newly elected President Eisenhower approved an additional $385 million in aid to South Vietnam.

Ho Chi Minh's forces, with the aid of Russia and China, defeated the French, a year later, in 1954, and France withdrew from French Indonesia. President Eisenhower wanting to keep the spread of communism in check after World War II, and with the departure of the French, sent increasingly more aid and military advisors to South Vietnam. This involvement in Vietnam was inherited by JFK and, subsequently after his assassination, passed onto President Johnson.

The first acts of aggression between North Vietnam and the US Military were initiated by the North Vietnamese Navy when on several occasions they fired torpedoes at US ships patrolling in the South China Sea. The north was resupplying its VC forces in the south by docking small boats in coastal villages along the South China Sea. In 1964, President Johnson used this attack to pass legislation, giving him broad powers to combat the growing insurgency in Vietnam. The legislation was called the Southeast Asia Resolution and was passed overwhelmingly in the House by a vote of 416 to 0 and in the senate by 98 to 2.

This was a critical time for the United States on the world stage. Our allies had to know they could depend on America's resolve and resist the threat of communism. The United States had just been humiliated at the failed Bay of Pigs invasion of Cuba, and Russia was the first to launch into outer space. Russia held onto most of the land it had occupied during World War II and was now looking to Asia. Aside from Vietnam, at the same time, communist's insurgents were trying to topple the governments of Malaysia, Burma, and the Philippines.

PROXY WARS

Our patrols would frequently encounter enemy soldiers which would result in brief firefights. Charlie infrequently engaged US soldiers for very long, choosing rather to attack and retreat before we would call in artillery or air support.

During the Tet Offensive, our primary support was 155 mm Howitzer artillery or Huey Blackhawk Helicopters. Huey's (or *birds* as we called them) had a door gunner on each side manning an M60 machine gun. The M60 machine gun is a belt-fed, automatic-firing 7.62 caliber weapon with a rate of fire of 500 rounds per minute. Occasionally, the Hueys were also fitted with rocket launchers.

The Blackhawk was the workhorse of Vietnam, used for air support, transporting troops, infantry insertions, resupply, and medivacs. Later in 1968, the Huey Cobra was introduced into the I Corps. The Cobra was designed as an attack helicopter with close in infantry support in mind. It was particularly adept for quick and silent attacks and to secure landing zones. Structurally, the Cobra had a narrow configuration and room only for the pilot and copilot. The armament for the Cobra was eight TOW anti-tank missiles, two rocket pods, one under each wing each housing nineteen 70 mm rockets and a 7.62 three barreled minigun in the front turret.

Khe Sanh was situated fifteen miles south of the DMZ west of Hue and about six miles east from the Laotian border. General Westmorland had established the base as an anchor for the Northern part of South Vietnam in I Corps. Khe Sanh and the A Shau Valley were close to the resupply routes of the Ho Chi Minh trail, which supplied the communists of I Corps with reinforcements, supplies, and communication. However, President Johnson (LBJ) refused to let the US take any military action against the enemy outside the borders of Vietnam. He was fearful that it would be interpreted by the Chinese or the USSR as an expansion of the war and may lead to their public commitment and outright support of Ho Chi Minh. Johnson was too afraid of public opinion and did not want the American people to know that we were engaging the Chinese and the Russians, as we had done in Korea, which had ended in a stalemate.

The truth of the matter is that, after World War II, both the US and the USSR had nuclear arms capabilities. However, neither country was ready to engage the other in a war for fear it could escalate into a nuclear war. Russia was determined to implement communism throughout the world, and the US sought to check the spread of communism. The US and the USSR fought proxy wars to implement their respective strategies. The proxy wars were fought in Korea 1950–1953, almost

Cuba in 1962, Vietnam 1962–1973, and the US support of Afghanistan after the Soviets invaded in 1979. The war in Israel in 1967 could have been another proxy war; however, the US backed Israelites defeated the Soviet-backed forces in six days. The current proxy war in Syria has the US covertly supplying the Al-Qaeda rebels, while Russia is arming both the Assad Regime and Iran who is overtly supporting Assad.

The unexpected victory of the cold war was the bankruptcy of the USSR. The communists, however, have never given up their goal for world domination. They will use any country or people to accomplish this one overriding goal. This explains the support Russia and China give to Iran, Hezbollah, Syria, Hamas, and the civil wars of genocides in Africa. It is all reminiscent of the policies and strategies used in Vietnam, Cambodia, and Laos. The communists provide arms and support to a rebel force and let the indigenous population kill each other off. When the civil war is over, the communists install a communist regime.

KHE SANH

On January 20, the NVA attacked the US base at Khe Sanh. This was both a diversionary tactic preceding the Tet Offensive and an attempt to overrun the base, from which the NVA would support its war effort after the victory of Tet. Charlie hoped that the resources poured into Khe Sanh would divert resources from the Tet Offensive, thereby, weakening the US's ability to respond to the offensive.

Ho Chi Minh had also duped the fearful and indecisive LBJ into a cessation of the bombing of North Vietnam from January 27 until February 3. Ho had told LBJ that the halt to the bombing would prove the US could be trusted and then he would enter peace negotiations with the US. Ho's real motive was to stop the bombing so that his troops and supplies could be moved into the South to support the Tet Offensive. General Westmoreland was able to convince LBJ to resume the bombing although the cease fire was almost over.

Because LBJ refused to allow US forces to engage the enemy in Laos or Cambodia the US Special Forces recruited members of the Hmong population to support us in our efforts from within Laos and Cambodia. Hmongs also lived in the jungles of Vietnam in tribal villages, they were known to us as Montagnards. Originally, the Hmong people were from China, and, being fiercely independent, they fled the oppressive Chinese regime and settled in remote areas of French Indonesia. The Hmong were promised US citizenship after the war for their participation and assistance with the US military. However, a lot of them were left behind, and did not immigrate to the US.

Initially, the Ho Chi Minh trail had been a foot path; however, with the US commitment to South Vietnam, China and Russia stepped up their aid. China and Russia sent road building equipment to Vietnam to help transform the footpath into a major road capable of handling all the supply trucks and tanks they were giving to Ho. Laos and Cambodia being off limits the construction of the trail went on unabated.

TET

The Tet Offensive was launched on January 31 1968. It was conducted primarily by the VC with support from the NVA. Tet affected almost all of South Vietnam with attacks launched against 160 towns and villages, including the Imperial City of Hue and the capital of Saigon. The communists had control of the city of Hue initially. However, in the thirty days of battle before they retreated, they never were really in complete, unopposed control. The marines and the ARVNs, particularly the ARVN Black Panthers, remained in the city for the duration of the battle.

In February of 1968, after the Tet offensive had been launched all across South Vietnam, the O-Deuce was stationed along the Perfume River to stop NVA reinforcements and supplies from entering Hue. Troopers of the O-Deuce also apprehended many of the NVA that were trying to escape from Hue. Most of our engagements were night ambushes when the enemy (either NVA or VC) would try to circumvent US positions to gain entry into the city. However, the O-Deuce was seldom where Charlie thought we were.

During the day, we would run scouting missions in our immediate AO. Often, the scouting missions would yield caches of enemy supplies, AK47 assault rifles, ammo, rice, mortars, crew served weapons and medical supplies. We often found tunnels and tunnel networks that ran for miles, housing supplies and enemy soldiers to support the siege of Hue. The tunnels also housed underground hospitals. The tunnel networks in some instances around Saigon and Hue were extensive and ran for miles.

The tunnels were built by the Viet Minh while they were fighting the French. The warfare of the communist revolution was a hit and run campaign against the French. When the French withdrew from Vietnam, Ho's Viet Minh forces began their insurrection against the government and people of South Vietnam. The Viet Minh using guerilla tactics attacked ARVN forces and tried to destabilize the government. The Viet Minh also perpetuated terrorist attacks against the populace of South Vietnam. This type of covert warfare necessitated all of their activities, supplies, food, and medical facilities to be underground. The tunnels provided the protection for all of the supplies and munitions that were being smuggled in from the north.

At the end of February, the O-Deuce, along with other elements of the 101st and 1st Cavalry, surrounded Hue and converged on the city. The South Vietnamese Army and the Marines had been primarily responsible for defending and retaking Hue. Tet was the first major offensive of the Vietnam War. Tet was a last ditch effort of the communists to starve off defeat as in many previous wars, not unlike the Battle of the Bulge at the end of World War II.

During the time the communists infiltrated Hue, they systematically assassinated doctors, lawyers, politicians, professors, and prominent citizens. The bodies of some 2,800 citizens of Hue (termed *enemies of the state*) were found in shallow mass graves after the communists withdrew.

The Tet Offensive was a military disaster for the communists. Our losses were 1,500 US soldiers killed and 2,500 ARVN's killed. Of the estimated 80,000 Vietcong, 45,000 to 50,000 were killed and another 7,000 were captured. The Vietcong never recovered from their losses, which forced the NVA to take a more active role in the conflict.

One night, after Hue had been secured, I was making rounds when I happened upon an orphanage staffed by nuns. Most of the kids in the orphanage were children whose parents had been murdered as, *enemies of the state*, in the genocide committed by the communists. I felt so bad for these kids. There wasn't much I could do. I handed out some of my rations. The kids wanted me to stay. One little girl brought a book over to me wanting me to read to them. I took the book and kind of sounded out the words to a couple of stories. The kids smiled and laughed and kept laughing, I thought they were just laughing at my pronunciation. After a while, the nuns told the children it was bedtime. When I was leaving, one of the nuns thanked me for reading to the kids and said the lighthearted stories were good for them to hear. She asked me where I learned

Vietnamese, I told her I could not speak Vietnamese. She said that my reading was in perfect Vietnamese. So I guess if I ever spoke in tongues, this was it. The little girl that brought me the book did not want me to leave. I tried to adopt her, but the US military will not allow unmarried GIs to adopt children.

FIRST STRIKE

1st Battalion of the O-Deuce was named *First Strike*. we were the modern day equivalent of the Calvary. Whenever US forces were in need of infantry support, we would be choppered in, as an insertion team, to provide that support. No matter where we were—at An Lo, Sally, or in the field—if fellow soldiers or ARVN's were in trouble (and if we were not engaged with the enemy), we would be choppered in for support.

We were also the first response team to downed helicopters. We would attempt to arrive at the downed bird before VC could arrive to take our pilots prisoner. The first time I was on a helicopter rescue, our bird landed and I ran over to the crash site. I looked inside to see if the pilots were still alive. Both of them were dead. The top of the pilot's head was severed off and his brains were laying in the glove compartment. That picture is etched in my mind forever.

During helicopter insertions, we either flew in to support other troops in position or we landed behind the opposing force to catch them in a cross fire. This call was made by the troops on the ground. We hoped it was an NCO making the call, not a second lieutenant. These rapid assaults usually had one of two outcomes; either we knocked the hell out of Charlie or they disappeared into tunnels.

Of the seventy-six helicopter insertions I made, fifty-four of them were into hot LZs. A hot LZ meant the choppers would be coming in under gunfire as they tried to drop off the troopers. They would not land the birds, they would just come in, swoop down low to the ground, and pause while we jumped off. There were times we would lose a trooper or two coming into a hot LZ. On rare occasions, we would lose a bird. After the insertion, the pilots would take off using evasive maneuvers to avoid further gunfire. A helicopter can be brought down by rifle fire.

There are several situations where we would anticipate a hot LZ, like coming into an area surrounding a village where US or ARVN troops were engaging the enemy. We would come under fire as we approached a village that was a VC stronghold. We also frequently came under fire as we were being inserted into the A Shau Valley.

We received intelligence that the VC had heavily infiltrated a village on the outskirts of Hue. As we were being choppered in for an insertion in the immediate area of the village, we noticed a lot of activity in the village. The lead bird made a quick pass over the village, there were a lot of people running around and this is unusual. However, we did not take any ground fire.

Our first four birds landed and we disembarked. As we started to move into the village, we received small arms fire. It was from more than just a couple of weapons. We advanced and brought in more troopers. In short order, we had a sizable force on the ground and the resistance was still very heavy. We started taking casualties, so we called in for a gunship. The resistance increased, it looked as if they were reinforcing at a rate faster than we were. We pulled back and called in an air strike. Charlie could often reinforce his position with soldiers that could join the fight from the tunnel network.

An airstrike is an incredible experience to watch. Jets, usually F-4 Phantoms would come in about a thousand feet above us at about five hundred mph. The F-4 would swoop down to about five hundred feet to insure accuracy when they dropped their bombs. We would use either napalm or High Explosive (HE) weighing 250, 500, 750 or 1,000 pounds.

Bomb detonations are a release of an incredible amount of energy. After a bomb exploded, I would see the shock wave move out from the source of the explosion as it compresses the air and the humidity. When the shock wave reached where I was standing, I could feel my clothes press up against my body. The Hollywood versions of a bomb going off are in actuality about 10 percent of a real bomb explosion. A one thousand HE bomb will leave a crater about twenty-five meters across, depending on the type of soil. After the airstrike, we secured the village and found ninety-six dead VC.

After the Tet Offensive, we were sent into the jungles to help relieve the marines that were under siege at

Khe Sanh. Khe Sanh and the A Shau Valley were major obstacles for the NVA; they were located very close to their main supply line, the Ho Chi Minh trail. The NVA also wanted to possess Khe Sanh and the A Shau Valley to use as staging areas for men and supplies for future operations. They desperately wanted to remove the US threat from their AO. There were rumors that we were going to parachute into Khe Sanh. However, that reminded everyone too much of the French defeat at Dien Bien Phu, so the plans were scrapped. So instead of jumping, we travelled on foot.

We moved from the foothills into the jungles west of Hue. The NVA were massing troops for a major offensive against Khe Sanh. Six thousand marines (with the aid of airstrikes and artillery weather permitting) were able to hold their ground. The siege of Khe Sanh lasted seventy-seven days, after which, the enemy retreated in defeat.

Tet and Khe Sanh were the major engagements everyone was waiting for, so that we could inflict heavy casualties on the enemy and force them to the negotiating table. We did not understand at the time that the communist regime did not care how many of their soldiers were killed.

I have seen estimates that the NVA had anywhere from 50,000 to 150,000 troops for the siege on Khe Sanh with casualties and fatalities as high as 50 percent. It was hard to be certain because of the density of the jungles; there was almost no ground visibility. Charlie was very good at taking their dead and wounded away and hiding the bodies. Troopers found ropes tied to meat hooks that the NVA would use to retrieve bodies from the battle field so we would never really know how many had been killed. They knew we used KIAs (killed in action) as a measurement of our success in a war of attrition.

It wasn't until after the war we learned how devastating our campaigns had been to the communists, one million killed in action against the US and ARVN forces. But when your people are just tools, it doesn't matter what the losses are. Stalin killed twenty-six million of his people; Mao did about the same. Although the numbers were smaller, Ho Chi Minh was no different than his contemporaries.

When the NVA attacked Khe Sanh, US artillery dropped shells on both sides and right through the middle, splitting the force in half and boxing them in. The shells walked the front-half of the force up to the perimeter and into our defenses while the back-half turned and fled right into our airstrikes.

Tet and Khe Sanh were significant victories for the US and ARVN forces, the enemy in both encounters were devastated. The communists would avoid any further major engagements with the US and would, from then on, rely strictly on guerilla tactics.

FRIENDLY FIRE

En route to Khe Sanh, Bravo company of about 125 troopers was moving along a foot path, heading west on the left side of a ravine. To our right, there was a formation of NVA moving towards us on the other side of the ravine that separated us.

Small arms fire broke out and a firefight ensued. Knowing we were heavily outnumbered, our forward observer (FO), a second lieutenant, called in for artillery support. However, all of the artillery within reach was engaged with the siege of Khe Sanh. The FO opted for the less effective 81 mm mortars from a firebase close by.

The FO called in the mission, and because we were already engaged, and because of the close proximity of a largely superior force, he requested the mortar crews to *fire for effect* on the map coordinates he had given them. There were no test rounds for accuracy.

Mortars tend to be less accurate, because you don't aim them like artillery per se; the distance for the projectile is set by the amount of gun powder used to the fire the weapon. This is always a tricky proposition when you are dealing with hills and ravines which make estimating the flight path of the trajectory of the mortar round difficult.

I was the second man in the second squad of the second platoon. All of the mortar rounds fell short and landed directly on our position. The mortars inflicted heavy casualties on the first platoon and the first squad of the second platoon. After we had given orders for the mortar team to *check fire* no one dared move. We knew we had sustained heavy casualties and were in less of a position now to engage the enemy. We took a position of waiting to see what the enemy would do.

As we lay there, the screams and cries of my fellow troopers became too much for me to bear. I knew we would have to medivac the wounded or many of them would die from their wounds. I grabbed my M16 and a machete and ran to a level patch of ground and began hacking out an LZ for the medivacs.

This was March 26 1968. There were eleven laying dead and nineteen that were severely wounded. When people are wounded by explosive devices, such as grenades, mortar rounds, artillery shells, or bombs, the sheer force of the blast blows limbs off the torso. Secondly, are the wounds inflicted by shrapnel from the shell casing. Additionally, when an airborne explosive device hits a tree or other objects they get blown into pieces. The pieces then become deadly projectiles.

I do not remember how long I was cutting down trees and underbrush, but everywhere I turned, there were more body parts. One Trooper was screaming for someone to bring him his leg that had been blown off. I saw a boot where the leg had been severed flush with the top of the boot. There was also someone's face hanging in a bush.

After a while, other troopers came out when they saw that I was not taking any fire from the enemy and began to help cut the LZ. Now, the pressure was off me, others were helping, and I just became overwhelmed by the carnage. I went into shock.

I was trying to grasp the images of people being blown into pieces. Why did they have to be blown into pieces? I started yelling to God, "Why?" A trooper grabbed me and sat me down by a tree, he told me to just stay seated. I did not know at the time I was in shock, because you do not realize it until it's over. When you are in shock from sensory overload, everything does seem to move in slow motion. I remember that as I sat there, still trying to acclimate to what I had just seen, I just kept repeating to myself, "All I wanted to do was to help people." I consider this to be my lowest common denominator. When you're in shock, nothing else matters except contending with what has put you on overload, all that is top of mind is one thing to hold onto: mentally.

There is absolutely no way to train someone for this kind of an experience. It is simply unbelievable. As was often, the case when Charlie knew we had support, either air or artillery, they would abandon the area and the fight. Charlie had a great respect for the accuracy and abundance of our firepower. The LZ was cleared and the medivacs were called in; the wounded were taken out first, then the dead, then the survivors.

We were taken to a nearby firebase, and, in one of the many ironies of war, we were taken to the firebase that had just fired the mortar rounds on our position. That kind of a meeting between soldiers is just impossible to describe. It was a horrendous experience, for both sides, and it was an accident. The good intentioned, erroneous act of one man, eleven dead and nineteen maimed for life.

The next day, we were choppered back to LZ Sally to await reinforcements to get us back up to fighting strength.

Life is terribly unforgiving of any carelessness, incapacity, or neglect, especially in war.

TAKING POINT

It was pretty well-known by this time that the January Tet Offensive was one of three such planned attacks. The next was to occur on May 5, and the third, sometime in September.

In anticipation of this while we were waiting to get back up to strength we conducted platoon size helicopter insertions into suspected enemy strongholds or into villages known to have an enemy presence. We wanted to provide as much interdiction to the resupply efforts of the NVA as we could.

A Blackhawk Helicopter could hold ten troopers with all of their gear. An insertion could be anywhere from a squad to a platoon. If it was a major operation, and the whole company was involved, the troopers would arrive in waves. The choppers would come into their destination at low altitudes following the contour of the terrain that often provided us with the element of surprise.

By this time, my primary duty was *walking point*. The point man walks in front of the formation, depending on the terrain, anywhere from several hundred meters in the rice paddies to fifty meters or less in the jungle. The point man has several very important duties. First of which is to ensure you do not lead the formation into an ambush or an enemy position. I would watch for booby traps, enemy patrols, or positions, bunkers, tunnel entrances, and any signs of enemy activity. The point also sets the pace for the formation depending on the degree of danger. It can be perceived of as a guinea pig kind of a job because the main purpose is to warn the rest of the formation of any danger by putting yourself in the position of danger first. The average life expectancy of a point man in Vietnam was eleven days. That's about how long, on average, someone held that position before they were killed or wounded.

The most necessary skills for a point man to have are the ability to notice any movement and to notice anything that does not belong with anything else in the immediate area. The human eye is naturally drawn to movement, but a point man has to be able to detect even the slightest movement or as little as just a trace of something manmade. Manmade things or uncharacteristic shapes do not naturally blend into God's creation, no matter how well camouflaged. I am blessed with being very proficient in both of these skills sets.

One of my first experiences walking point I came upon a water monitor. I didn't know what a water monitor was; I just knew there was a six foot lizard on the path in front of me. I signaled for everyone to halt. Scotty came forward to see what the holdup was. When he asked me what was wrong, I pointed to the lizard and said, "What the hell do you do with something like that?"

Scotty walked over to the lizard, and with his foot he just pushed it down the embankment into the river. Scotty was one of those guys, that just always seemed to know what had to be done and when. Scotty was one of the few that survived his tour with the O-Deuce, one of the 3 percent.

The operations we conducted into surrounding villages were very successful. At times, the fighting was fairly intense; however, the firefights never lasted too long. Charlie was adept at a tactic we called *shoot and scoot*. They would engage us with small arms fire, and when we counterattacked they would disappear into tunnels or fade into the dense foliage.

They would also leave behind booby traps, which accounted for a lot of our fatalities and casualties. Booby traps were concealed explosives devices, rigged with a trip wire, when someone tripped the wire, the explosive device would detonate. The explosive device could be a grenade, a mortar round, and artillery shell, and even bombs. Charlie also used pungy sticks, which were sharpened bamboo steaks smeared with human feces and positioned so that if you had to dive for cover you would land on the pungy sticks. They would also dig holes and place a .50 caliber round inside on a striking pad so when you stepped on it, the bamboo covering the hole it would give way and the weight of your foot would set off the round. A .50 caliber round is capable of removing a limb. This same configuration of the covered hole was also used to conceal pungy sticks.

Three times while I was walking point, I hit a trip wire and was able to *sense* the wire and stop moving so that the booby trap did not detonate. I would then indicate to my shadow the location of the booby trap so it could be disarmed. I also stepped on the bullet traps twice and stopped my foot before it made contact with the round or the pungy sticks.

Once, as we were coming into An Lo for a break, we were fairly close so some assumed we were safe. I stopped and a new guy who was impatient to get to An Lo passed me. He went about fifteen meters and tripped a booby trap. His shrapnel injuries were sufficient to necessitate a return to the states for treatment and rehabilitation. US and ARVN troops never employed the use of booby traps as we never knew where our troops would be traveling.

Both sides made extensive use of ambushes. Charlie moved at night so we ambushed at night. We moved during the day so Charlie ambushed during the day.

The first time our squad was ambushed, I slipped out of my rucksack and slid down a small embankment and low crawled through some weeds to a hedgerow. Low crawling is pushing yourself along on your belly with your feet and pulling yourself with your elbows while your rifle is cradled in your arms. I then crawled through the hedgerow. When I came out on the other side, Scotty was also emerging from the hedgerow. We were the only two that survived the ambush.

We were ambushed again a couple of days later; this time, I was the only one to survive. By the end of the year, I will have survived six ambushes.

One night on ambush, I had a position to the flank of the main body. Flank positions in an ambush were set up so that you could not be approached from the back or sides without warning the others. An enemy formation was coming into our kill zone when I noticed the formation had three people walking flank on my side. They were going to miss the kill zone and were approaching right where I was posted. I didn't know if anyone else knew they were there. I readied my M16 but knew I could not shoot until the ambush started.

The ambush was started by the lieutenant throwing a hand grenade at the three men on flank. I emptied my M16 and reloaded; however, no one was returning fire. The main body was in the kill zone when the grenade went off and most of them were killed by small arms fire. In the morning, I looked for the three men on flank and all I found was a foot.

Another time, we were set up on a trail and a single VC came down the trail. You don't want to spring an ambush for a single person. Doing this will reveal your position and the ambush may miss the opportunity for a larger force. However, he noticed us lying by the trail, and, thinking we were VC, he squatted down and started talking to us. This was the one exception to the don't-ambush-one-person rule.

Walking point was too intense of a job to do every day so we rotated. I would usually walk point every third day or under special circumstances more frequently. These were the better-let-Newman-take-point situations. The longer the time you spent on the line, the more proficient you became. In short, some people became really good at what they did. I became really good at walking point, nothing passed my notice.

On the days I didn't walk point, I would sometimes be a tunnel rat. This is one job I absolutely hated. It was just plain intense fear. I often would have to go into the tunnel with my M16 that was impossible to maneuver in a tunnel. I wrote my dad and asked him to send me a revolver; however, before he could send it, I had taken a 9 mm pistol from a dead Chinese captain I found after one of our ambushes. A handgun in a tunnel is much more manageable. By this time, I was down to about 125 pounds, with a good tan, and black hair, so in the darkness of a tunnel I could be mistaken for a Vietnamese, which may give the enemy pause—and a pause, sometimes, is enough.

If that's not a clear image, imagine a tunnel rat that weighs 175 pounds, is fish belly white, and has red hair, or an African American for that matter—instant identification.

In light of all of this tunnel-rat business, when someone asked me if I would walk point for them, because they had a "bad feeling about that day," I was more than happy to oblige them. Don't get me wrong, there were times on point that were extremely stressful and dangerous as well; you're just not trapped in a tunnel. Sometimes, if the tunnel situation just appeared too perilous, I would throw a grenade into the tunnel before I went in.

On my third day, I would either walk shadow for the point man or pull LP duty at night. LP is a listening post. When the company sets up for the night, four listening post are posted outside the company's perimeter. These positions are early warning posts to defend the perimeter and warn the company of any impending danger.

One night, we could not make radio contact with the LP to our left. A couple troopers from the company's position low crawled out to check their position. All three of the troopers in the LP had their throats slit. One of them had apparently fallen asleep while on guard duty. Charlie had crept up on them and killed them.

When you're in position for the night, one person takes a two hour guard duty watch and two troopers sleep. This roster rotates until morning, two hours on duty, and four hours of sleep. Needless to say after this episode, I would pull guard duty all night and let the other two sleep. I knew I could trust myself not to fall asleep.

324B NVA

By April 19, we were back up to strength and had orders to head back into the mountains to Bastogne for operations in the A Shau Valley. Bastogne was within striking distance of both Khe Sanh and the A Shau Valley. We were also able to call in fire support from the USS New Jersey. The New Jersey had sixteen-inch guns that fired a projectile weighting 2,700 pounds, and had a range of twenty-three miles. The rounds were so big that you could hear them whistle as they flew overhead.

En route to Bastogne, we were traveling by foot through the foothills, heading to the jungles that covered the mountains in the western portion of the I Corps. We were walking in company formation with the three point men, one from each platoon taking the lead. First platoon's point was at the head of the formation, as point for second platoon, I was on the left flank, and point for third platoon was on the right flank. We were in rice patties, so we were well ahead of the company.

We came to a point where two hedgerows converged in front of us, forming a V. The enemy could fire from the full length of both hedgerows; and as long as they fired on line, they would not shoot each other. To avoid shooting your own men, ambushes were usually set up in an L shape. These two hedgerows provided an excellent ambush site. I thought this would be a perfect place for Charlie to ambush our company.

As soon as I realized the ambush potential of the hedgerows, I did an immediate left face and headed for the hedgerow on my left. As soon as I had gone about fifty meters, I made someone very nervous, and he opened fire on me with his AK-47. I immediately dove to the ground. As soon as I hit the ground, a mortar round exploded to my immediate left, no more than five feet from where I was laying. The blast from the concussion knocked me unconscious.

Typically, when we or they initiate an ambush, it is started with either a grenade or a mortar round. The ensuing explosion is meant to surprise the enemy and give notice for everyone in the ambush to open fire at once. If the ambush is not started this way, and someone just begins shooting, the element of surprised is compromised and there is enough time for evasive actions.

Because of our forward position, the company was able to withdraw before they were in the kill zone of the impending ambush. Unfortunately for me, everyone thought the mortar round had been a direct hit on me, so the company pulled back assuming I was *pink mist*.

When an individual sustains a direct hit by a mortar, an artillery round, a substantial booby trap, or near a bomb for that matter, the explosion just vaporizes the person—pink mist. It is called pink mist because the combination of five quarts of blood and 150 pounds of disintegrated white flesh; and all of our flesh is white, just appears as a pink mist.

The first time I saw pink mist, I was walking as a shadow for a new guy learning how to walk point. I thought he missed something, so I stopped to take a better look. Once my curiosity was put aside, I looked up to see how far ahead of me he was. Just as I looked up, he tripped a booby trap. There was a tremendous explosion, and I saw him transform into pink mist. There were little pieces of flesh caught in my web gear.

The mortar round on this particular morning, after the aborted ambush, went off about 10:00 AM, and I regained consciousness just before dark. I had no idea where our company was or if the enemy was still in the hedgerow. I low crawled in the opposite direction we had been headed for about two or three hundred meters, then got up and ran full throttle in the direction I thought our company would have gone. After a while, I stopped running and tried to figure out where the company would most likely be positioned.

I was scared. It was getting dark, and my two biggest fears while in combat were being taken prisoner or losing a limb. Right now, I was a prime candidate for either of these two scenarios. It is almost impossible to detect a booby trap in the dark.

As night set in, it was a clear night, so visibility was good. As I moved along looking for the company, I heard a couple of shots. I also noticed about a quarter mile away the glow of the end of a cigarette. I knew it must be Americans. I headed in that direction and was confronted by an LP. The troopers in the LP asked me for the password, which I was able to give them. It was Bravo Company.

Once inside the perimeter, I was congratulated for a job well done as the ambush had been averted. I was also given the nickname *Lucky*, because of my many near misses and especially for this one. I was told to report to the medic to get checked out. While I was sitting with the medic, I explained what had happened. I also commented on how loud the crickets were. The medic told me there weren't any crickets. He said, "You hear crickets because your ears have been blown out from the concussion and don't expect them to go away, they won't." And they haven't. The shots that I had heard as I was coming into our position were snipers. They were targeting troopers that were smoking at night and not cupping their cigarettes. The sniper had scored two kills that night.

We were continually harassed by snipers. A favorite tactic of Charlie's was to snipe at a formation, and when a fire team was sent to take out the sniper the team would walk right into an ambush.

It is unfortunate that snipers were viewed so negatively by so many in the US. A sniper is a valuable resource and every infantry squad should have at least one. One time, as we began to move from our night position, I led out as point and had not gone very far. When I heard a distant report of a rifle, I then heard the round from a sniper's rifle zip past my head.

As we were moving out the morning after the aborted ambush, we came under small arms fire, which immediately grew in intensity. It was obvious from the fire superiority of the enemy that we were heavily outnumbered. We returned fire and mounted an offense. We also called for a Huey gunship and artillery.

When the firefight was over, our CO called for reinforcements. Alpha and Charlie Companies from the O-Deuce joined us that morning, bringing our strength to about 425 troopers.

An infantry company at full strength consisted of about 164 Troopers. An infantry platoon had three rifle squads of ten men each and a light machine gun squad of nine. The machine gun squad was two teams, and each team carried the M60 machine gun. The companies are usually designated: Alpha, Bravo, and Charlie. Each platoon squad was divided into two fire teams. Each squad has a sergeant in charge and a corporal or SP4 (specialist fourth class) in charge of one of the fire teams. Each platoon has one lieutenant, first or second, and a platoon sergeant, a radio operator (RTO) and a medic for a total of forty-three troopers. The company also has a first sergeant, an FO or forward observer, a company commander who is a captain, his executive officer, and their RTO. We would usually operate anywhere from 100 to 150 troopers.

If we got much below one hundred, we could be called back into base for reinforcements, but that was the COs discretion. There were many variables, recent activity, recent losses, impending mission, and amount of enemy activity that the CO had to consider. When we were called back, we would usually run squad or platoon size patrols out of the base.

Our recent firefights began the day after the aborted ambush and would turn out to be thirty-three days of straight combat with major elements of the 324B Division of the NVA. Sometimes, we would get involved in skirmishes as elements of each side ran into each other and, sometimes, it was an all out gun battle as we each tried to out maneuver and outflank each other. It is a very unnerving sound to hear the enemy have fire superiority in a firefight, because you know you are outnumbered and vulnerable to a superior force.

One afternoon, I heard a firefight breakout; as I proceeded to the sound of the fight, I came upon a staff sergeant, E-6. He was laying next to a log and he told me to take a position on his other side. He wanted the log on one side of him and me on the other. I told him, "The fight's not here, it's over there, let's go." I never saw him again.

In major conflicts, we would call for artillery or Huey Cobras for support. One time, the pilot of a Cobra mistook us for the enemy and strafed our squad. The bullets missed us by inches. I watched the ground erupt under the bullets inches from our feet as we were lying at the base of a hedgerow.

I think the reason Charlie continued this engagement, instead of breaking off as they usually do, is that they knew our strength and they knew theirs. The soldiers in the 324B numbered about three thousand, and when they saw us in the open walking to the hedgerows, they knew we were just company strength. I think they thought they would quickly overwhelm us with their superior numbers. However, superior firepower is a decisive advantage in a battle, so is tenacity and the American will to win.

One day, we were engaged in a firefight that lasted about an hour. I ran out of ammunition—very scary and very dangerous. All you can do is ready your grenades and fix your bayonet. Fortunately, I found enough ammo lying around from fallen troopers to get me through the end of the fight. From that day on, I carried four hundred rounds of ammunition; double the required amount.

After one of the numerous firefights, one of the medics asked me if I would take a wounded trooper to the evac LZ. He had been wounded in the head and his bandage covered his eyes. I lead him over to the LZ. When we got there medivacs were taking some of the wounded out. The medics had about twenty troopers they were trying to stabilize. There was also a row of about fifteen body bags waiting for transport once the wounded had been flown out.

I went back for more wounded, trying to hold back the tears. This is why freedom and liberty are such precious ideals, and only those who truly understand this understand that these are not just ideas, but ideas worth dying for in order to guarantee their preservation. I think some people do not understand this because they are too far removed from the price that some pay to realize that this is what freedom and liberty costs.

We had one trooper that was terrified of the thought of a sucking chest wound. The wound is called a sucking chest wound because a bullet or shrapnel has pierced the chest cavity and entered the lung. So you breathe out of the closest passage, which would now be the hole in your chest. It makes an awful gurgling sound, and they require immediate medical attention in a facility.

For the most part, I don't use names in most of this because I don't know who will eventually read it. So this trooper gets hit, and it was a sucking chest wound, we told him it's not and that his wound doesn't look too bad and all of that. A medic new to our platoon comes over and radios for a medivac. He is told the medivacs are very busy and they will get to him when they can. He said he needed a medivac now because he has a sucking chest wound. As soon as the trooper heard that, he went into shock and was dead within a minute. The power of the mind in provisional reality is a force that needs to be realized and reckoned with.

At the end of thirty-three days, the fighting was over. We had taken 257 prisoners, and the enemy body count was 2,382 killed in action. I do not know how many troopers we lost as those numbers weren't available. Replacements kept coming in, replacing fallen troopers, and you would hear that someone didn't make it. Sometimes, after a firefight you would ask about someone and all a trooper could say was, "Sorry, he got hit and was medivaced, but it doesn't look too bad or I don't think he'll make it."

There are stories for every one of the thirty-three days of contact; they all just start to run together. The frequent firefights were brief and very intense, major battles could last for an hour. Each side would try to

inflict as much damage as possible in the first few minutes. We would dig in and call for help. Charlie would
put up a good fight and then disperse. All that remains
to memory of this engagement are snap shots of scenes,
not the sequence of events. Gunships working a hedgerow; a napalm strike; field first aid; seeing someone shot
or blown up; making a ditty bag, which is tying off the
sleeves of a tea shirt to make a bag to hold someone's
intestines so the they don't get contaminated; emergency tracheotomies, and so on and on and on.

An oddity of war is that a trooper begins to become
very selective about who they choose as a friend.
Because of all of the truth and honesty, you get to know
people very well. Truth and honesty are the glue for
any meaningful relationship; none of these are casual
relationships. However, friends may not be around very
long, so you get selective about whom you let in. I didn't
let myself get close to guys that, through discernment,
I felt would not be around very long. These were guys
that thought they knew it all, big ego's, guys that lacked
common sense, and guys that just weren't very bright.
I don't know if it is right or not, it's just the way it was.
I knew I had erected an emotional firewall, and I wondered what the residual consequences of that would be.

When my daughter, Ariel, was born, she had colic,
which is a condition marked by recurrent episodes of
prolonged and uncontrollable crying and irritability.
She would wake up every couple of hours at night crying. One time, when I was holding her trying to quiet
her, I looked at this one month old who had not done
anything at all yet, and I was struck by how much I

loved her. It made me think how much, in spite of ourselves, that God and Christ love us. Not because of anything we do, but because of Their tremendous capacity to love.

All of the surviving members of the O-Deuce received a Bronze Star from the US and the Vietnamese Cross of Gallantry from the President of South Vietnam for decimating major elements of the 324Bth Division of the NVA. The 324B had also been participants in the battles of Hue and Khe Sanh. After the battle, we were sent to LZ Sally for a break and to get back up to strength. When we arrived at LZ Sally, we were a little miffed to see that even the cooks and clerks in the rear, who never see combat, had been given a Bronze Star. But when a general says, "Decorate the whole outfit," that's what happens.

Another oddity of war is, after surviving a firefight, one that has been particularly intense, I wanted so much to laugh. I guess it's just a release, but it feels very strange. I couldn't laugh; troopers had died, and I survived. I suppose this goes along with the phenomena of survivor's guilt. This troubled need to laugh is depicted by Christopher Walken in the movie *Deer Hunter* while he and Robert DeNiro, as prisoners, are forced to play Russian roulette. I think this reaction is caused by the realization that you have just survived something that you never thought you would.

The first personal battle to overcome in combat is fear. I left America and flew to a foreign land. When I arrived, all that I owned was in my rucksack and my weapon. There was nothing to prepare me; there is no amount of training that is adequate to prepare a soldier for battle except battle. Nothing else can be so horrendous, so shocking and so unbelievable. That is why the side with the most seasoned troops is always at an advantage.

A battle, almost always, begins suddenly with someone being shot or blown up, a sudden explosion. A trooper needs to get over that right away so that he can react appropriately. However, the event is so violent and so unbelievable it takes a few seconds to realize what has actually just happened. The suddenness and the horror of the event take a while for the mind to process the situation. It is necessary to just shake it off and come back to it later when things have quieted down, when the immediate threat is over. Some people just freeze up and can't function. I guess it's just fear.

During the onset of an engagement, if a soldier is well trained, or better yet, experienced, reactions are automatic and occur without much thought. So how does a soldier conquer fear? I had to just force myself to do what I had to do—no matter what. You have probably heard it said that "there are no atheists in foxholes." What that means is that a soldier needs strength outside of himself.

I know the one thought I had that brought me through all of my experiences was the thought that *God would not be putting me through this if He didn't have a reason*, so I just trusted God in all of it. I think trusting God gave me the ability to push myself to do what I didn't think I could do and enabled me to do things that I was afraid to do. There are people that can muster the courage to do what has to be done and there simply are others that cannot. The world is full of average people, and average people will never make a difference in their life or in the lives of others. I think the operative factor is faith in God, something to believe in beyond yourself.

There are those who after repeated success, just like the Israelites, think it is all of their own doing and they forget God. Fear often comes from not knowing if you can accomplish whatever is required. However, with each success, one gains more confidence and resultantly becomes less fearful with each subsequent engagement. I learned to trust God more; because in a war, truer words were never spoken than those recorded in *Proverbs*, "Mans steps are ordained by the LORD who can understand his way." (Proverbs 20:24 NASB)

People that are fearful tend to get scared, which produces more fear—it is a downward spiral. Fear can also make a person over cautious, which in itself can be a liability for oneself and for others.

There is another element to all of this. When I knew I was going into a hot LZ, there is time for reflection about the upcoming danger and I could get a little anxious. However, it's different when it just starts unexpectedly, people either seek cover and protection or they get fired up. When I would get fired up, I wanted to get into the action. I wanted to do my best, I wanted to make a difference, and I wanted to make sure our side won. People that are courageous, as God has asked us to be; focus on what has to be done and not on their fear. They do what is necessary and leave the outcome in the hands of God.

A couple of observations from the battlefield. We had many conversations about God, war, death, pain, and suffering. It was my experience that Christians die bravely, that is to say—without fear. Non-believers were terrified of death. In spite of what Hollywood would have you believe, no one calls out for mommy just before they die. People do, however, cry out for *Jesus*.

When someone dies, you can tell immediately that their soul has left their body and you can tell it from fifty yards away. It's like a light turns out. We all have this aura around us that we cannot see, but you notice its absence when it is gone at death. The Hollywood depiction of taking someone's pulse to see if they're dead is ridiculous. It's an immediate transformation from flesh to clay.

As a side bar to training, one day—fifteen years after I returned from Vietnam—I was changing my daughter's diaper. When I was at the changing table, my back was to the bedroom door. My wife came home from work and I did not hear her come into the house. She came into Ariel's bedroom walking up behind me. Because of the *crickets* in my ears, I did not hear her. She put her hand on my shoulder. The next thing we both knew, she was upside down in the corner of the bedroom.

A SHAU VALLEY

After our engagement with the 324B and a brief stay at LZ Sally, as we got back up to strength, we resumed our march to Bastogne. We were well into the mountain jungles and I was walking point, Canailles was walking shadow for me. As I turned a bend in the path, I was face to face with a squad of NVA regulars. I fired my M16—and nothing—it misfired. Canailles jumped up to my side and began firing his weapon. The enemy dispersed. First squad went into the bush on both sides of the trail, but the jungle was just too thick, the enemy slipped away. I don't know why they did not just open fire on me.

There was a lot of criticism about the M16, and there were some problems with it early on. When the M16 was first authorized for the military, it came with a specified gun powder to be used. Somewhere along the line, the gun powder was changed and this is what caused all of the empty case extraction problems. When the unauthorized powder ignited, it would expand the brass case so much that the ejector could not pull the empty shell out of the chamber to cycle in a new round. The empty shell case would become so jammed in the chamber that it would have to be pushed out with a cleaning rod, which was not supplied with the weapon. This case extraction problem did have a cost in American lives.

The army blamed the problem on soldiers not adequately cleaning their weapons. The gun powder was changed and new production rifles had chrome chambers. This rectified the problems; however, the stories and rumors continued.

The old M16s also had a three pronged flash suppressors on the end of the barrel. This was a constant irritant as the flash suppressor would constantly get hung up in the vines or underbrush in the jungle. We use to call them *wait a minute vines*, because you would have to stop to untangle the end of the barrel. The new production rifles also closed off the end of the flash suppressor. So that this was no longer a problem.

The M16 was a finely machined rifle, it also got a lot of use, and they frequently got wet. Like any firearm, they had to be maintained; if they were, they functioned flawlessly. The M16 has a very small projectile 5.56 mm or .223 caliber. The smaller the diameter of the projectile, the more accurate the round will be. The smaller caliber also produced very little recoil. This meant that it was easy to stay on target even when firing the rifle on automatic.

This was the only time my M16 malfunctioned. The one time, however, made me lose confidence in my weapon, so I ask for and received a new one. Point has to have 100 percent confidence in their weapon or any

infantryman for that matter. My new issue rifle was a
new production version. Eventually, all of the M16s
in the O-Deuce were replaced with the new ones:
the M16A1. We joked that we got issued new rifles
because Lady Bird Johnson was a major stock holder in
Colt Arms Manufacturing.

The jungles of Vietnam are a triple canopy jungle.
This happens when a growth of trees is established; a
second growth has to pass the first one to reach sun-
light, then a third. It is so humid in the jungles that
leeches live on the leaves of the underbrush. They sense
you when you walk by, and they stretch out to try and
grab hold.

While I'm on the subject of leeches, we had to cross
many streams, canals, and rivers. Once you emerged on
the other side, a couple of troopers would keep watch
while everyone took their turn dropping their trousers
and pulling off the leeches, sometimes as many as a
dozen. Like every other insect in Vietnam, in the triple canopy jungles, the insects are huge. One time, I
missed a leech, and that night, my leg was itching like
crazy; when I scratched the itch, it felt sticky. I pulled
a poncho over me and lit a match, my leg was covered
in blood from the knee down; the leech had sucked so
much blood it exploded. I still have the scar to this day.

The jungles were also the home of Mr. Two Step,
as we called him, which is a pit viper snake, lime green
about an inch in diameter and less than two feet long.
The rumor was that if a person were bitten by Mr. Two
Step, you would live long enough to take two steps
before the venom killed you. I stepped on one once

without realizing it and just stunned it. My shadow however, went crazy. I heard this commotion behind me and looked back to see what was going on. My shadow was frantically smashing the snake with the butt of his rifle to make sure it was dead.

There were also centipedes in the jungle that were a foot long, red and black, with pincers on their head; they were also very poisonous. The first time I saw one, we were sitting down for a break, and Canailles told me not to move; and then pointed out that a centipede was walking past my hand. I froze, it walked by, and Canailles slammed it with the butt of his rifle, it didn't flinch, it just kept walking into the underbrush.

There was also a time when I woke up and I just knew something was wrong. I did a very slow sit-up and looked back to where I had been sleeping. Two scorpions had nestled into my armpit for warmth during the night. In the field we always slept on the ground. Whether it was in the excessive heat of summer or the cool constant rain of the monsoons, we slept on the ground. Exposure to cool damp weather never makes anyone sick, it takes a germ, pathogen or a virus to make you ill.

One day, as I was on point and we were a couple of miles from Bastogne, an observation helicopter sighted an enemy ambush at the top of the hill we were approaching. The CO kept the company back and sent me ahead to scout out the hill. As I walked up the hill, my knees were actually shaking; it's like the knee cap is shaking. That had never happened before and it felt kind of strange. I reached the top of the hill, and Charlie must have decided against the ambush because of the observation helicopter, there was no one to be found. I walked back to where I was in sight of the company and gestured for them to come ahead. As they rose, I yelled, "Tanks," and they all dove into the underbrush. I walked down the hill and asked what the matter was, and they asked me if I saw tanks. I said, "No, I yelled 'Thanks.'" It was all I could do to keep from laughing. I don't know why this seemed so funny to me, maybe because they had just experienced a small fraction of what I had experienced. Payback.

We arrived at Bastogne and were going to participate in a joint operation with the 501st and the First Cavalry in the A Shau Valley. Bastogne had 105, 155, and 175 mm Howitzers as well as 81 mm mortars to provide support for excursions into the A Shau Valley. The 105 would fire a 33 pound projectile a little over 7 miles. The 155 fired a 43 pound projectile a little over 9 miles and the 175mm fired a 147 pound projectile 23 miles. Khe Sanh was out of range for the artillery at Bastogne, but we could supply helicopter support and troops.

The 1st Cavalry was going in on the Laotian end of the valley and we were going in the other end. These operations in the Valley were called the hammer and the anvil. A superior force was inserted at one end of the Valley and they would push through the Valley. This was the anvil. The other force, smaller and more mobile, would run excursions up the Valley towards the anvil. These were the hammers.

Charlie would think the hammers were looking for caches and bunkers, unaware we were driving them into the anvil. I don't know why they never seemed to catch on to this, as it always worked, with varying degrees of success. As we moved towards the anvil, we would encounter resistance when we came close to caches that Charlie did not want to give up. After the firefight they would retreat towards the border. When we pursued, they would cross the border into Laos where we were not allowed to pursue and they had a safe haven. So we would put an anvil in their path.

When they ran into the anvil, the hammer would continue its advance and we would squeeze them in the middle. This was a very effective strategy, as the communists always fled to their out of country sanctions when confronted by the US Military. During our battles at the A Shau Valley, the NVA had their command structure and their artillery in Laos, which they used with impunity.

DEPARTMENT OF THE ARMY
Headquarters 2nd Brigade, 101st Airborne Division
APO San Francisco 96383

AVDG-BA   22 June 1968

SUBJECT: Presentation of the Vietnamese Cross of Gallantry with Palm

Troopers of the Second Brigade

On 19 June 1968, Vietnam's Armed Forces Day, the 2nd Brigade Task Force 101st
Airborne Division, was presented with the Vietnamese Cross of Gallantry with
Palm by the President of the Republic of Vietnam Nguyen Van Thieu for its'
outstanding performance in the coastal plains area in the vicinity of Hue,
Thua Thien Province, during the period 19 April 1968 to 10 June 1968. The
citation accompanying the decoration pointed out the successful operations
conducted by the Brigade in Quang Dien District against VC and NVA forces, its
defense of Hue, and the successful rice denial program conducted throughout
the Brigade's area of operations. It further mentioned the destruction of
major elements of the 324B North Vietnamese Army Division and cited the following enemy casualties and captured weapons during the period:

    2382 VC and NVA killed in action

    257 VC and NVA captured

    724 weapons captured of which 119 were crew-served.

The presentation of the Vietnamese Cross of Gallantry with Palm to the colors
of the 2nd Brigade is a great honor and a tribute to the courage and dedication
of every man in the 2nd Brigade Task Force. I am very proud of each one of
you and of the job you are doing here in Vietnam.

This award must now be processed administratively through both Vietnamese
and U.S. channels. It is unknown at this time if this award entitles the
units of the 2nd Brigade Task Force to display the Vietnamese Cross of Gallantry on their respective colors, or how individual awards will be authorized.

                             J. H. CUSHMAN
                             Colonel, Infantry
                             Commanding

Laika and me

Scotty (center left) Myself (center right)

Denny

Orphanage in Hue

An Lo Bridge

Chopper insertion

REAL COLLATERAL DAMAGE

Prince Norodom Sihanouk was the President of Cambodia and tried to walk a fine line by claiming to be a neutral country in the conflict in Vietnam. However, Sihanouk was pro-communist and allowed the NVA secret sanctions within his borders. He allowed the construction of base camps and supply depots.

Whenever the US or ARVN forces had Charlie on the run, they would head for the sanctions of Cambodia and Laos as President Johnson refused to let us cross the border. When South Vietnam fell to the communists, to show their gratitude, the communists ousted Sihanouk from power and replaced him with a communist ruler more to their liking Pol Pot, who they later disposed of as well. Pol Pot killed one and a half million of his people in Cambodia that were *enemies of the state*. His murderous reign was so outlandish that anyone who wore glasses was considered part of the *intelligentsia* and therefore eliminated. This is documented in a movie called *The Killing Fields*.

And we all remember the *boat people*, the desperate effort of the South Vietnamese to flee from the new communist regime. When South Vietnam fell to the communists, an estimated 800,000 people were killed as *enemies of the state* and by 1990, 750,000 Vietnamese had fled to the US. More than a million fled to other western countries.

Laos at the time was pro-democracy and allowed the US to bomb the Ho Chi Minh trail that ran through its boundaries. However, the country was divided and the northern portion, parallel to I Corps, was sympathetic to the communists. In essence, Laos was a sanction for the NVA as well. The US, however, did bomb the trail on the border with Vietnam in Laos.

Most of the Hmong population wound up in Laos after the war. The South fell to the communists, and soon after, the communists invaded and took over Cambodia, which forced the Hmongs into Laos. The communist South Vietnam then invaded Laos and toppled the government clamming it as a communist's state. This forced the Hmong into Thailand. The exodus became so great that Thailand did not know what to do with all of the refuges. Australia and the US took some of them. Thailand tried to repatriate them and send them back to Laos; however, they were persecuted, murdered, and imprisoned by the communists. Their plight goes on to this day. The last major effort was to bring 15,000 Hmong to the US by a bill proposed by the US House and senate; however, then President Bill Clinton said he would veto the bill if it was passed. Special provisions were made under the presidency of

George Bush, and many were allowed to immigrate to the US.

Hmongs remaining in Laos are persecuted to this day, especially those who helped the US and their descendants. There is a documentary that profiles the plight of the Hmong's called *Hunted Like Animals*. Because of the inability of our president and the congress to act decisively and boldly with a strategy to win the war millions of people were killed and millions more were displaced. If the same people had been in charge during World War II, we would all be speaking German today.

After the Tet Offensive, Khe Sanh, the initial forays into the A Shau Valley, and similar victories at the same time in II and III Corps, the VC and NVA soldiers were decimated. If President Johnson had used the same bombing strategy employed by President Nixon under Linebacker I and II, and if the sanctions would have been lifted against our ability to attack targets in Cambodia and Laos, we could have won the war in the summer of 1968.

The United States lost 58,229 soldiers fighting in Vietnam over the course of ten years and was defeated by the purse strings of a reluctant president and a liberal congress. In all actuality, the US was not defeated in Vietnam; we left after a negotiated settlement in 1973. South Vietnam fell to the communist two years later. However, we did not leave a presence in Vietnam as we did in Korea. There was too much perceived anti-war sentiment in the US. The domino effect that the liberal left said would never come about—that

Laos and Cambodia would fall into the hands of the Communists if we did not win in Vietnam is exactly what happened.

The United States soldiers in Vietnam never lost a battle of any consequence. In the three-day battle of Gettysburg during the Civil War, there were 56,000 casualties and fatalities on both sides, the North and the South. Personal sacrifices for ideas which people were willing to die for brings meaning and life to these ideas. As a normal course of life, about 50,000 people die in the US every week. Each year, our traffic fatalities in the US average about 40,000 deaths. There is no honor in death on the highway. We also abort about one and a half million babies every year in the United States. Where is their Constitutional Right to life, liberty and the pursuit of happiness? Abortion is not pro-choice; the choice for murder has already been made. Why is there so little concern over the lives of aborted babies?

American losses in Vietnam were 58,229. The South Vietnamese Army lost 260,000 soldiers. The Communists, between the Vietcong and the North Vietnamese Regular Army lost one million killed in action. Why are there always those that protest the defense of freedom, rights, liberty, and dignity of peoples that are oppressed?

One reason, people are so adamantly opposed to war is because of fear. Those that have experienced war and behaved cowardly cannot reconcile to themselves that they conducted themselves in a manner that was less than honorable, so they protest the war. The rationale is that war must be so terrible, that is why they behaved as they did. Because of pride, it does not enter their mind that it was a matter of their lack of intestinal fortitude. There are also those so terrified by the thought of war they protest in hopes they never have to go into battle.

Granted not everyone has the mettle to engage in an armed conflict, but that is no reason to denigrate those that do. The truth of the matter is that those who answer the call to defend our nation and its interests are a different breed. They are all heroes from the soldier to the policeman to the firefighter. This country is blessed in that every time our national sovereignty has been challenged, we have about 10 to 15 percent of the population that is willing to step forward to defend the United States of America and its ideals.

There were 2,888,800 Americans that served in uniform in Vietnam, representing 9.7 percent of that generation. 58,229 were killed in Vietnam, 75,000 were severely disabled, and 23,214 were 100 percent disabled, 5,283 lost limbs, and 1,081 sustained multiple amputations. There are still 2,338 Americans unaccounted for from the war. Ninety-seven percent of Vietnam veterans were honorably discharged, 91 percent say they are glad they served and 66 percent say they would do it again, even knowing the outcome. Although exact statistics vary from source to source these numbers appear to be consistent across most sources. The statistics recorded here are from a 2007 VFW (Veterans of Foreign Wars) magazine article; *Vietnam Warriors: A Statistical Profile.*

Vietnam era veterans have lower unemployment than the same non-vet age group, and on average, they earn 18 percent more in income than their peers. Vietnam veterans are also less likely to be incarcerated; only one half of one percent has been in jail. Vietnam veterans were the best educated forces our nation had ever sent into combat; 79 percent had a high school education or better. Service men from well-to-do areas had a slightly elevated risk of dying because they were more likely to be pilots or in the infantry. Almost eighty-seven percent of the men who died in Vietnam were Caucasians, 12. 1 percent were black, and 1.1 percent were other races. These percentages also approximate the proportions of those involved in the war. Two-thirds of the men who served in Vietnam were volunteers as opposed to two-thirds of those that served in World War II were drafted. The average age of US troops in Vietnam was nineteen. The average age for World War II GIs was twenty-six.

As we readied for the mission into the A Shau Valley, we would run patrols out of Bastogne, consisting of a squad, usually about twelve men. After a couple of days, we began running into more and more of the enemy on our patrols, enemy concentration was building.

Firefights are very brief in the jungle; it doesn't take long to distance yourself in such heavy cover. When the Army Corps of Engineers built Bastogne on the hill top, they cleared the perimeter out from the base for about three hundred meters, creating a kill zone.

One night, Charlie tried to overrun the base, the firefight became very intense. Charlie liked to get as close to our position as they could before they started their engagement as they wanted to be so close, that we could not employ artillery or other support elements without endangering our own troops. The NVA assaulted Bastogne about midnight.

We would occasionally shoot off an illumination flare, just so we could see what was going on and to keep Charlie off guard. It was as we fired one of these illumination flares that we saw Charlie low crawling through the kill zone, trying to sneak up on our perimeter. We engaged the incoming infantry with all that was available, claymores, mortars, grenades, .50 caliber machine guns, M60 machine guns, and M16s, of course. We were being particularly aggressive as Charlie had recently employed the use of flame throwers, and we did not want them close enough to use their flame throwers.

Just a few days before, while engaging Charlie in a firefight, we had lost two troopers to their flame throwers. Being burned alive is a horrible way to die. As they advanced, we continued to fire illumination rounds, which lit up the kill zone.

I had taken a position next to a bunker and was firing at Charlie with my M16. The guy on the bunker next to me was manning a .50 caliber machine gun. He was hit by enemy fire and taken out of action. A .50 caliber machine gun is too valuable of an asset to have sitting idle during a firefight. When he was hit, I dropped my M16 and manned the .50 caliber. I waited for illumination rounds to explode and would mark a target, or I would fire two rounds at what I assumed to be a potential enemy position. The fire fight probably lasted twenty or thirty minutes before Charlie retreated in defeat. Firefights just seem like they last longer because so much happens in such a short period of time.

The next morning Bravo Company was to move into the A Shau Valley, however, Charlie Company was sent in first instead. Often times, the orders were changed based on who had the most recent contact and which company had the highest number of combat ready troops. Bravo Company had fared less well on the previous night's attack, so Charlie Company was sent in ahead of us. By the end of the day, Charlie Company returned by helicopter, sixty dead and sixty wounded. The remaining ten troopers were assigned to Bravo Company. Bravo Company went into the Valley the next day as the hammer. I don't think there was a single trooper in the O-Deuce that did not know the 23rd Psalm by heart.

Hollywood typically portrays the most accomplished soldiers as being a little crazy, and it's implied that it's what it takes to be a warrior. That portrayal could not be further from the truth. The best soldiers are men of faith, men that believe in what they are fighting for, with a high regard for the sanctity of human life, and possessing exceptional moral fiber.

Intelligence had determined that Charlie was getting ready for the second wave of Tet or the *mini Tet*. After we completed the hammer and anvil operation with the 1st Cavalry, we were pulled off Bastogne and sent back to the vicinity of Hue.

By this time, I had been with Bravo Company for seventy days and was the third oldest man in the platoon. That's not a measurement of age that means only two troopers had been in the platoon longer than I had. The other forty of our original compliment had either been killed or wounded, along with many replacements. I would spend another 180 days in the field.

The offensive called mini Tet was just that it could not really be considered an offensive at all. The mini Tet amounted to some rocket and mortar attacks on installations. However, there were no ground assaults, and no towns or villages were captured. The VC just had too few people to mount an offensive, the 324B Division was gone, and many others had been killed at Tet, Khe Sanh, and in the A Shau Valley.

In case all of this is confusing, the O-Deuce, the 1/502nd of the 101st Airborne Division, spent most of its time between Hue, the coastal plains north of Hue, and the A Shau Valley. When we were in the coastal plains, we conducted village operations where we secured villages, village by village. Our normal activity while we were running our missions was to look for VC or NVA, signs of activity, offering medical assistance to villagers, and inquiring about enemy activities. Locating and destroying caches of food and supplies. Routing out the VC and assuring villagers of their safety, engaging the enemy whenever the opportunity presented itself, and responding whenever we were attacked. We also frequently set up night ambushes. After we had secured the village and removed whatever VC presence had been there, PFs would be assigned to assure continued stability of the village.

By far, the majority of the Vietnamese we encountered were grateful for our presence and our assistance in helping them preserve their freedom; the ones that were not appreciative were VC or VC sympathizers.

One time when we were on a stand down at An Lo, a local *papa san* wanted to express his appreciation for all that we were doing, so he wanted to souvenir us dinner. I don't know how the word souvenir came to mean to give something to someone, but that is what it meant. Two other troopers and I went to his hooch for dinner. Just as we were finishing, the MPs were making their rounds, so *papa-san* showed us out the back door. As we were leaving, I noticed a freshly butchered dog close to his hooch. I asked him what had happened, and he said, "*Papa-san* souvenir GI number one…chop, chop." The meat in the rice we had just eaten was dog. Just don't ask me how it tasted, "Run, Spot, run."

CHIEU HOI

One day, we took prisoners in a village, and some of them were fourteen and fifteen years old. We had our *cowboy*, inquire as to why such young men were taking up arms. The interrogations revealed a new recruiting technique employed by the VC and NVA to try and replace their forces that had been decimated by US and ARVN troops during the fighting of Tet.

Every couple of miles, there were ricing villages. There might be as many as twenty hooches, straw houses that housed a family. The families would farm the rice patties within walking distance of the village. Beyond this village would be the next village, and so on.

After our cowboy had interrogated the young prisoners, he told us the VC or NVA would come into a village and would call everyone out into the center of the village. Then they would execute the chief's youngest child by shooting them in the head. They would then tell everyone that if the men did not come and fight with them, and fight honorably, they would come back and kill everyone. The men were then sent to Hanoi for indoctrination.

The statistics I saw on these recruitment executions were that approximately 4,000 children were assassinated. Statistically, on average the victims were four years old, and more often than not, they were female, about the same age as the little girl I tried to adopt from the orphanage. You probably have the same question we did: What kind of a person can shoot a four year old child in the head? What's the catchphrase? Man is basically good?

Why was this never reported in the news? Because the executions would give credence to the cause of the US Military and would run contrary to the progressive agenda. At its most basic level, wars are fought when there is no other way to stop the shedding of innocent blood. These were the kind of stories the American journalists ignored, they were way too inexperienced in covering a war. Previous wars were covered by military journalists. The military journalists were accustomed to battle and understood our mission and our cause, which was reflected in their reporting.

Walter Cronkite was on the way out, and the journalists were trying to make a name for themselves. The big story had to be of maximum interest to Americans, and what wrong we were doing, shock value, to elevate their status. Their interest was not reporting the news.

Everyone remembers the picture of Vietnam's national police general holding his revolver to the head of a VC prisoner just before he shot him. The picture made the photographer famous. What the reporters failed to report is that the VC that was shot had killed the general's entire family, and his second in command, the day before. I'm not saying it was right. I question, in a war zone, what I would have done if I had been in his shoes. There are two things to fear most: Someone with everything to lose and someone with nothing else to lose.

Because of these recruitment executions the US implemented, the *Chieu hoi* program translated *open arms* into the I Corps. Word was spread in the villages and pamphlets were dropped telling the VC that if they yelled *Chieu hoi* and surrendered their weapons, they would be well treated and reunited with their families.

The realization of these recruitment executions also had a profound impact on us troopers. We took a completely different view of our enemy; our resolve migrated to one of compassion and understanding for the VC. There were hardened NVA that took advantage of the program, but our cowboys, could always tell the difference. Some of the NVA *Chieu hois* actually became Kit Carson Scouts or cowboys for the US.

A word about cowboys, these were Vietnamese soldiers that volunteered to work with the American troops. Somewhere along the line, they had seen movies of the great American west; they had a six-gun in a holster on their hip, a cowboy hat, and a red handkerchief around their neck. If any of the cowboys performed really well, GI's would give them a cowboy vest. Then he would be the envy of all of his peers. The cowboys were an invaluable asset when it came to our prisoners. They knew the language and the customs. The NVA that became cowboys knew people, places, and methods of the NVA. They also knew who the enemy was, often times, we could not tell the difference between a VC and a civilian. The VC were well integrated with the local population. We did not have anyone proficient enough in Vietnamese to interrogate our prisoners, so we had to send them to the rear for interrogations. This cost valuable time, and in many instances, could jeopardize our ability to immediately respond to situations. The cowboys were more aggressive in their interrogations than we would have been, and they could tell if someone was lying. I never witnessed this, I only heard about it. If a cowboy had some particular hard cases that would not reveal any information about their activities, the cowboy would take them up in the helicopter. He would ask questions, and if nobody talked, he would throw one of them out of the helicopter. Word had it, that after he had thrown one of the prisoners out of the helicopter he couldn't shut the other ones up.

One time, I was walking point with our cowboy, and I stepped on a python. I could tell it was large by how big it felt when I stepped on it. The python took off and all you could see was the grass swaying back and forth as it made its retreat. The cowboy pointed at the grass moving and said laughingly, "GI step on python, and python *dee dee mow*," which means to go away quickly. He said, "Vietnamese step on python, python crocodile Vietnamese." Crocodile means *to kill*.

DON'T BOMB
ANYTHING IMPORTANT

The bombing of North Vietnam had once again been suspended as a goodwill gesture for the peace talks. And again, we were overrun with NVA soldiers. We could predict that every time the bombings were suspended, a week later, we would be in firefights just about every day.

President Johnsons bombing campaign called Rolling Thunder was restricted from bombing anywhere close to Hanoi or the Haiphong Harbor. There was a Russian ship anchored in the harbor so Johnson had the bombers stay clear of the harbor. Because Johnson's bombing campaign was so restrictive, it did very little to aid the war effort.

In August of 1967, then Governor of California Ronald Reagan said the, "US should get out of Vietnam," explaining it is difficult to win a war in which "too many qualified targets have been put off-limits to bombing."

Ho used the peace talks as leverage to suspend the bombings so he could further infiltrate the South. Not long after Rolling Thunder began, Ho told Johnson that if he stopped the bombing, he would entertain the prospect of a negotiated settlement. Johnson stopped the bombing, and during the lull, the Soviet Union installed the most sophisticated anti-aircraft batteries that the world had ever seen up to this point in time.

US pilots were not allowed to bomb Russian MIG aircrafts that were sitting on the ground. American pilots became so frustrated over all the restrictions that one day some F-4 pilots scrambled their jets and, as bait, assumed a bombing run formation. The Russian pilots assuming they were making a bomb run scrambled into their jets to shoot down the bombers. If the jets were on a bombing run, they would be very light on defensive munitions because of the weight of the bombs. When the MIGs engaged the F-4s, seven of the MIGs where shot down in twelve minutes without one US plane even being hit.

President Nixon's bombing campaign called Linebacker I and II did more in a few months than Johnson program accomplished in three years. Nixon's campaign forced the North to the peace talks and to negotiate seriously. When the North Vietnamese walked out of the peace talks, Nixon launched Linebacker II. The North Vietnamese peace delegation was back to the table in eleven days. However, we made too many concessions just to get out of Vietnam. This was a disservice to the entire SEATO (Southeast Asia Treaty Organization) signed after World War II, and the signatories of subsequent agreements, to assist nations under the threat of a communist takeover with a promise of mutual defense.

In the most basic terms Vietnam was not an unjust war, the US and other allies were honoring the treaties they had signed to mutually protect and defend Southeast Asian countries being threatened with a communist takeover. There was the SEATO agreement, the Truman Doctrine and the Mutual Defense Assistance Agreement, what is unjust is for a country to not honor the agreements they have signed.

The US was not the only nation to send troops to Vietnam. South Korea sent 50,000 crack soldiers, Australia sent 55,000. Troops were also sent by New Zealand, the Philippians, and Thailand.

A word about the soldiers from South Korea, they were called ROKs (rocks) which stood for the Republic of Korea. All of the ROK soldiers were trained in martial arts. They had also fought the communists in their own war of independence against communist aggression from North Korea and continue to live under the threat of hostile aggression from north of their DMZ. The ROKs were very aggressive and decisive in battle. When they took prisoners, the prisoners were subject to very harsh interrogations; many of whom did not survive. The ROKs were stationed in II Corps and the region they were in saw the least amount of enemy activity. The VC and NVA didn't want to have anything to do with the ROKs. A lesson America can learn, when you are in a war, your sole intention should be to win. Ultimately, this strategy saves lives, both civilian and military.

Ho had spent some time in France and understood how public sentiment could sway the policies of a free society. He used that to his advantage in the conflict in Vietnam. Ho travelled to France in an attempt to convince the French to just leave French Indonesia without a war. While Ho was in France his second in command Vö Nguyên Giáp, later Ho's general, in typical communist fashion, killed or imprisoned all of Ho's opponents.

General Westmoreland believed that if enough of the enemy were killed, we would reach a tipping point where the communists could no longer be able to sustain the fight. Americans have a very low tolerance for battlefield deaths, no matter how significant the cause. The communists simply did not care how many people died, soldiers or civilians. Communists are godless people and have no regard for the sanctity of human life.

This is best put into perspective by considering that any impropriety by a US soldier is dealt within the strictest of terms. Whereas, the communists are treated as warriors and heroes for their countless atrocities, which our media failed to report. I don't think it was an unpopular war as much as it was a mismanaged war from Washington and dishonestly reported by the media.

One day as we were operating as a LRRP, we encountered a superior force. They had set up an ambush that was started prematurely; we set up defensively and engaged them. We tried to advance as fire teams, but the resistance was too strong. Fearing being overrun, we pulled back and called for support. 1st Platoon from Bravo Company was choppered in, and we resumed the offensive. We were able to overrun their position. Most of the NVA were killed, some ran off and we took a few prisoners. The medic went in with some troopers to tend to the wounded and retrieve the bodies of those who had fallen.

I was escorting a couple of prisoners when I heard from the medic that "it looks like they tried to skin one of our guys." That was more than I could take, and I proceeded to knock the hell out of one of my prisoners. He feared for his life and ran off into the rice patties and disappeared into a hedgerow. Yes, I lost my prisoner, I just got angry; you do not shoot children in the head and you do not skin people.

SUICIDE BOMBERS

It was during this time of so much infiltration of the enemy from the north that LZ Sally was attacked. Just after dark, the guards on the perimeter bunkers heard rockets being fired, so they yelled *incoming*. Once the firing is heard, you have, at most, a few seconds—depending on how far away they are—to respond. Incoming is yelled when a forward post hears the *thump* of the launch. Unlike the Hollywood version where rounds are landing around everyone and the protagonist will yell *incoming*. They are not incoming—they are there. As if no one knew there were incoming rounds with explosions going off everywhere.

Charlie fired the rounds to create a diversion and to get as many troopers as possible into the bunkers for protection. The rockets were fired to break holes in the barbwire that surrounded our perimeter. After the initial barrage, sappers broke through the wires. Sappers are essentially suicide bombers. They carry an AK47 or a handgun and a satchel filled with explosives. Once inside the wire, amidst the confusion from the rockets, they run through the base firing their weapons and throwing their satchel charges into the bunkers, tents, anywhere they anticipate there will be a heavy concentration of troops seeking protection from the incoming rounds.

I was in the compound when they came through the wire. With so many people running around, I didn't want to take a shot. I also knew I did not want to get into a bunker. I just lay down on the ground looking for an opportunity that never materialized. After they threw their charges into a bunker, they tried to head back to the perimeter for an escape. Several of the charges detonated in the bunkers, and there were quite a few killed and wounded. None of the sappers made it back out of the wire; they were taken out by the bunker guards on the perimeter as they tried to exit the base.

WE KNOW LOVE BY THIS

We know love by this, that He laid down His life for us; and we ought to lay down our lives for the brethren.

1 John 3:16

Bravo Company was in the field and was told to rendezvous with Alpha and Charlie Companies for support in taking a deserted village suspected of being an enemy stronghold. Alpha Company was attempting to move into the village. Their point man ventured in and tripped a booby trap and was killed. The CO sent in the next man, who was also killed by a booby trap. He then sent in the point man from Charlie Company, who was killed by a booby trap as was the second man sent in from Charlie Company.

By this time, Bravo Company had arrived. The CO told Bravo Company to send in their point man. Our platoon sergeant was Laika. He was a good friend of mine. We had sought each other out as we were both men of faith, although men of different faiths. We were both very interested in one another's beliefs. Laika was from British Somalia. We both knew what was coming; as point, I would have to go in.

Laika told the CO, "I won't ask my men to do anything I won't do myself." He headed for the village. About a minute later, we heard an explosion.

Because he was such a good friend, I was reluctant to go in.

Another trooper jumped up and went in.

I followed a couple of seconds later.

As I went in, the trooper came out, stopped me and said, "You don't want to go in there." He offered me a cigarette and said, "We'll have a smoke, and then call the medivac."

I exclaimed, "Let's call the medivac now!"

He looked at me, "He's lost both legs and both arms."

I lit my cigarette.

He told me that when he reached Laika, Laika looked at him and asked, "Are you guys alright?"

> "We know love by this, that He laid down His
> life for us, and we ought to lay down our life for
> the brethren"
>
> 1 John 3:16 (NASB).

After Laika's death, we refused to move into the village.

A senior battalion officer was circling above us in a helicopter. When he heard we refused to move, he had his helicopter set down so he could order or motivate us into moving into the village. Chances were that if the village was that heavily booby trapped, the enemy had already left, leaving the booby traps behind for us. His chopper landed, he disembarked and was immediately cold cocked by one of the platoon sergeants and thrown back on his helicopter.

That's how the story went, anyway. We were ordered back to LZ Sally to stand down.

We had orders to head back up to Bastogne for operations in the A Shau Valley. Our Company medic told the CO that I had lost so much weight that I should be looked at. They sent me to the hospital in Da Nang. I weighed 125 pounds, my normal weight was 145. I thought I was just sweating it off. The temperature averaged about 95 degrees and it would get as hot as 115 degrees by the afternoon. The doctor in Da Nang determined I had worms, and they treated me for that. After a couple of days of three hot meals a day, no stress, movies on the beach at night, and all the comforts of home, I was starting to feel a little guilty. I asked the doctor if I was okay. I was ready to go back. He told me I could stay there as long as I wanted to. I thought about it and told him, "No, I'd better get back."

When I returned to LZ Sally, Dennis, a very good friend, was in the MASH unit. He had lost his right leg below the knee. I went to see him, but what do you say to someone that has just lost a leg? I asked him how he was doing and he replied,

"At least, I'm getting out of this motherf——er."

I was grieved as I left Denny. In his opinion it was an okay tradeoff to lose a leg to be able to leave the fighting behind. So many had paid so much, and who would ever appreciate what everyone had done and what they had gone through. Who can possibly relate to what you have experienced when so much of it is hard to comprehend yourself? That's why so many do not talk about their experiences and that is unfortunate. With so much of the truth undocumented, ignored, or distorted the current generation just has Hollywood's and the progressive media's biased portrayal of what it means to be an American and the cost of freedom.

I also do not have much faith about what our kids are taught, or not taught I should say, in the public school system. It is the imperative responsibility of every American parent to make sure their kids are taught the truth about history, politics, and faith at home.

A case in point. A current history book explains the Mayflower Compact signed by the Pilgrims arriving at Cape Cod in Massachusetts as, and I quote.

> The Mayflower Compact was the agreement signed on November 11, 1620, by the male passengers on the Mayflower, before coming ashore, that they would form a body politic and submit to the will of the majority in whatever regulations of government were agreed upon. Its purpose, according to William Bradford, was to hold in check the restless spirits on board who had threatened to strike out for themselves when the Pilgrim leaders decided to land in New England instead of Virginia.

However, the Mayflower Compact actually says, quoting the original document,

In the name of God, Amen. We, whose names are underwritten, the Loyal Subjects of our dread Sovereign Lord, King James, by the Grace of God, of England, France and Ireland, King, Defender of the Faith, e&. Having undertaken for the Glory of God, and Advancement of the Christian Faith, and the Honour of our King and Country, a voyage to plant the first colony in the northern parts of Virginia; do by these presents, solemnly and mutually in the Presence of God and one of another, covenant and combine ourselves together into a civil Body Politick, for our better Ordering and Preservation, and Furtherance of the Ends aforesaid; And by Virtue hereof to enact, constitute, and frame, such just and equal Laws, Ordinances, Acts, Constitutions and Offices, from time to time, as shall be thought most meet and convenient for the General good of the Colony; unto which we promise all due submission and obedience. In Witness whereof we have hereunto subscribed our names at Cape Cod the eleventh of November, in the Reign of our Sovereign Lord, King James of England, France and Ireland, the eighteenth, and of Scotland the fifty-fourth. Anno Domini, 1620.

The purpose of the Pilgrims was to establish a colony for *the glory of God, and the advancement of the Christian faith*. However, your kids are not taught the truth in school, they are taught the lie. That is where your responsibility comes in as a parent and will remain so until the cowards are removed from public office. Many historians consider the Mayflower Compact as the prelude to the Constitution of the United States. If you change our history, you change who we are.

Patrick Henry, whose "Give Me Liberty or Give Me Death" speech has made him immortal, said: "It cannot be emphasized too strongly, nor too often that this great nation was founded, not by religionists, but by Christians; not on religions, but on the Gospel of Jesus Christ…"

Thomas Jefferson, chosen to write the Declaration of Independence, said: "I have little doubt that the whole country will soon be rallied to the unity of our Creator, and, I hope, to the pure doctrines of Jesus also." He proclaimed that it was the God of the Bible who founded America in his 1805 inaugural address; "I shall need, too, the favor of that Being in whose hands we are, who led our forefathers, as Israel of old, from their native land and planted them in this country." We cannot leave educating our children to a system pervasive with lies. Abraham Lincoln warned; "The philosophy of the school room in one generation will be the philosophy of government in the next."

Our missions in the Valley were twofold. We would look for enemy food, rice, and munitions caches and engage the enemy whenever we found them. Primarily, however, our goal was to rouse the enemy and drive them into the anvil. It is difficult to conduct operations in the jungles as the vegetation is so thick. Often, we would encounter resistance as we approached an area where food or munitions were being stored. Frequently, when you are in a firefight in the jungles, you are shooting where you think the enemy is because the vegetation is so thick you cannot really see the enemy.

On one of our missions through the Valley, we actually went into Laos, although we were not supposed to cross the border. We had come this far, had Charlie on the run and we were not about to give up the fight. When we had to report our coordinates, we were informed that we were in Laos in violation of our orders. We were ordered out of Laos, and back to Bastogne.

That night, I was conversing with one of my good friends. He told me "If you break a bone over here, they have to send you back home. Bones don't heal right over here."

I suggested to him; "I'll break one of your bones if you want me to."

He replied, "Would you really do that for me?"

I said, "No, I was kidding"

I went into the bunker to get some sleep. Then I heard this whack and a loud moan. I went outside and saw him with his leg propped up on some sandbags, an entrenching tool in one hand and he was rubbing his leg with the other. I asked him, "Did you break it?"

With a look of extreme pain on his face he shook his head no. I think his limp lasted for almost a week. We did have a couple of occurrences of self-inflicted gunshot wounds. Medics always knew the source of the injury granted there were accidents. We concluded the hammer and anvil in the Valley and returned to the coastal plains.

THE THRESHOLD
OF LIFE

Our next mission was on a suspected enemy encampment in a village in the coastal plains north of Hue. We came in on Hueys in whisper mode over the South China Sea and set down on the beach at about 3:00 AM. The plan was to wait until first light and then advance on the village and engage the enemy.

We started to move through the hedgerows surrounding the village just before dawn. The trooper next to me struck a wasp nest with the butt of his rifle. The wasps swarmed on me stinging me eleven times in the head and neck. The wasps are called Giant Black Wasps, and they were very large, about an inch and a half in length. The pain from the stings was so severe that as soon I was clear of the wasps I just sat down. I remember thinking I have never felt this much pain in my life. I called for the medic. He arrived; he saw the wasps and knew immediately what had happened.

Anaphylactic shock is a very serious allergic reaction including loss of consciousness, labored breathing, swelling of the tongue and breathing tubes, blueness of the skin, low blood pressure, heart failure, and death. Immediate emergency treatment in a facility is required. He told the CO I could go into anaphylactic shock from the wasp venom and needed to be medivaced. The CO told him we cannot bring in a medivac until the troops have engaged the enemy. His fear is that the medivac would give Charlie an early warning of our presence.

I'm not sure how long we waited. My eyes nearly swelled shut from my reaction to the venom.

I heard gunfire—M16s!

Punctuated with the sound of grenades exploding. This was followed by a delayed volley of AK-47s. Then I heard one of the most welcomed sounds of my life—the deep whisper of blades cutting through the air. Air Cav. Low and fast.

I had to be led to the chopper as my eyes were almost completely swollen shut. I love helicopters and this was one of the best rides I ever had. I looked at the gauges in the cockpit through the slits I had for eyes and saw that we were flying at 120 mph. We were moving along about ten feet off the ground. The ground was just whizzing by. It was incredible.

When we arrived at the MASH unit at LZ Sally, my eyes were completely shut because of the swelling caused by my reaction to the wasp venom. I had no facial features, and my face was so swollen it was completely smooth. I was placed on a gurney and rushed into the emergency room. When they brought me in, the doctor looked at me, with no facial features, and said, "What in the hell happened to him?"

I don't think he was sure how to treat me. When I heard his question, I realized a wasp had stung me in the mouth, and I had bitten down on it just to stop the pain. I pulled the wasp out of my mouth and held it up for anyone to see.

I then went into anaphylactic shock, and suffered a cardiac arrest and complete respiratory failure. I flat lined. As soon as I died, my spirit and my soul left my body. I just kind of floated up to the top of the operating room over the bed where my body was laying. The medical staff was administering shots of steroids and adrenalin into my shoulders. They hooked me up for a blood transfusion, in both arms. They put blood into one arm and drew it out of the other arm.

I was looking down at myself laying on the bed. There weren't any bright lights, there weren't any tunnels and there wasn't anyone there waiting to meet me. I was just above the operating table. There wasn't any fear or any concern, I was actually quite calm. It seemed if I was resuscitated I would go back into my body, and if not, I would just go somewhere else.

Why couldn't they see me? I could see them. I looked at my hand and it was translucent, I could see through it. They could not see me because I was translucent, and you cannot see something unless it reflects light. I was aware that I was fully conscious. It was still me, and I was still the person Tom Newman. As I looked at my body, it was as if my body was a glove and

I am the hand. As soon as I returned to my body, I lost consciousness.

The next thing I remember was waking up in the recovery room. I was astonished as I reviewed what had just occurred. I had just existed outside of my body. Frankly, it is very hard to believe it happened even when you know it just happened. Because you can hardly believe it yourself, the experience is so far removed from anything you have ever experienced. You wonder if anyone else will believe it really happened. I was thinking, *Okay, what was that? Was it a dream? Had I been in shock?* They were giving me shots; was it the effect of the drugs? But it all seemed so real, to real to have been a dream. But how could I verify that I had actually been alive outside my body?

The orderly was coming by making his rounds. The doctors rarely made rounds. They had more important things to tend to.

He looked at me and said, "Oh, I see you're coming around, how ya feeling?"

I looked at him and said, "Why were you guys putting blood in one arm and taking it out of the other?"

With a very surprised look on his face he said, "Man, how the hell do you know we did that, you were gone?"

That was what I needed to hear, if it had not been a real, conscious experience for me, how would I have known what procedures they use to resuscitate me?

> And they began laughing at Him (Christ), knowing that she had died. He, however, took her by the hand and called, saying, "Child,

arise!" And *her spirit returned*, and she got up immediately; and He gave orders for something to be given her to eat.

Luke 8:53-55 (NASB)

When I was able to get up, I went and paid a visit to the post chaplain, Chaplain Allen. We had had many good conversations about the role of soldiers in war. I asked him once how can Christians be involved in a war if the Bible says, "Thou shalt not kill" (Exodus 20:13 KJV). He said if your Bible says thou shalt not kill, it's a bad translation. The original Greek and Hebrew texts say, "Thou shalt not *murder*" (Exodus 20:13 NASB). There is a big difference. There is incredible evil in the world, and that is why governments are given the power of the sword. One of the roles of government is to prevent evil and the spilling of innocent blood. After my wasp incident, Chaplain Allen called me *Funny Face*; it wasn't until two days later, as the swelling was going down, that he realized who he had been conversing with.

When you die, it is like walking through a doorway, and as you cross the threshold you slip out of your jacket; it stays behind, and you keep going. At death, your body dies, however, we do not die.

It would be about twenty-five years before I would start to talk about my out-of-body, near-death experience to anyone but my family; and it was only after I was completing my twenty-year study of Scripture— only then—because everything was now starting to make sense. The most amazing thing that I remember from this experience is that in foundational reality; everything is the truth, there are no bad, wrong, evil or untruths, just purity and truth.

SEARCH AND DESTROY

I rejoined Bravo Company. We were on a mission to go into the *Cou Bang* desert and visit the villages closest to the ocean as these may be being used for resupply depots from sea-going vessels.

A lot of these missions into the villages were called search and destroy. We would search for enemy caches of rice, rifles, munitions, and crew served weapons. The caches were usually hidden in tunnels in and around the villages. Once we found them, we would destroy them. The tunnels were sometimes an area underground used just for concealing supplies and munitions. Sometimes, there were rooms or further tunnels past the area where the supplies were. There were also tunnels that led to underground hospitals or network of passages with various escape passages.

We used search and destroy tactics primarily, because in every major confrontation Charlie had with the US military, they were soundly defeated, usually by a ratio of ten to one. Because of Charlie's inability to defeat the US military, they relied almost exclusively on tactics of guerilla warfare—hit and run. This necessitated that they store supplies all over the countryside. Search and destroy was never meant as anything else, regardless of how sinister the press tried to make it sound. Take away their resources and they are less effective at engaging US and ARVN troops.

The news would talk about search and destroy missions as they showed pictures of US troops setting fire to hooches, implying that is what search and destroy meant. As far as I can recollect, we set fire to some hooches one time. The village had been long deserted and we conducted numerous missions into this village to rid it of VC, we finally just burned it. Search and destroy missions were to find and destroy supplies, weapons and munitions used to conduct war—nothing more.

There were several different scenarios for taking a village. In the *friendly villages*, the populace lived under threat of assassinations if they did not harbor rice and munitions for the VC. They actually wanted no part of VC activity but had little choice. When we would approach these villages, we would surround the village, and our cowboy would ask the villagers to come out. One portion of the formation would then begin a sweep of the village while the other troopers remained on watch in a blocking position. We would sweep through the village looking for caches of food and munitions. Sometimes, the VC would try to flee the village and would run into our perimeter. Otherwise, they would hide in their tunnels with the cache and hope that we did not find them. We were not always sure if we found all of the hiding places. We did not want to put the villagers in the position of having to show us where they were for fear of reprisals against them. Sometimes, we would locate the VC and coax them out of the holes. Then the cowboys would interrogate them to see if there were other locations. Sometimes, they refused to come out. We would fire our M16s into the entrance to the tunnel and that usually convinced them to give up. Occasionally, if they refused to come out or fired back at us, we would throw a grenade into the tunnel. Then someone would have to go in and see how extensive the tunnel was. There were times, however, when the villagers would discreetly let our cowboys know where VC were hiding. The friendly villages were taken by ground assaults only. Because most of the villagers were noncombatants, we did not want to use artillery or gunships that would result in collateral damage or the destruction of their village.

Other villages were dominated by VC, and we would take fire as we approached the village. We usually choppered to the villages to have the element of surprise. We would set a squad down behind the village and the rest of the platoon would come in from the opposite end. The ones that tried to flee were VC. In these situations, once inside the village, it was hard to tell who the enemy was and who was not. South Vietnamese citizens had been issued IDs that we would ask for; however, the VC had them as well.

Other villages were VC strongholds, and they would have run the local population out of the village. We would take heavy fire from these villages and these were the ones where we would call in artillery or airstrikes if the resistance was more than we could subdue because we were either outgunned or they were a superior force.

The real challenge is that some of the villages were somewhere in between. In these situations, our cowboys were invaluable at identifying friendlies from hostiles.

On occasion, we would move into an area on foot where we were going to conduct search and destroy missions and we would set up just before dark. We would dig shallow foxholes and go through all the motions of setting up for the night. Then an hour or two after dark, we would move out to either set up a night ambush or establish a perimeter around a suspected enemy stronghold, and sometimes we would do both. Then move on the village at first light.

The night before we crossed the desert, I felt like I was running a fever. I checked in with the medic, and he said my temperature was running a little high and to check in with him if I didn't feel better in the morning. The fever may have just been a residual effect from the wasp stings. The next thing I remember was waking up in the morning and saying to a trooper,

"I better see the medic before we cross the desert. I think I still have a fever."

The trooper replied, "What are you talking about? We just spent the last three days in the desert."

I didn't remember any of it. My fever had broken, but the medic said my temperature that morning was 103 degrees.

We approached a village on the outskirts of the desert and received small arms fire. As we advanced, the fire from the village became more intense and more plentiful. We had been informed that the village was deserted. We lost a couple of troopers trying to move into the village, and we encountered some booby traps, which took out a couple more troopers. We pulled back and called in an airstrike. I don't remember the body count from the village, but it had been a successful mission.

TYPHOON

Inclement weather was coming in from the ocean, and the expectation was that it may be a tropical storm of some magnitude. Choppers were sent out to bring the troopers of the O-Deuce into LZ Sally. They did not get to us before the weather got too severe and the choppers were grounded. This was during the monsoon season, which is the equivalent in Vietnam to winter in the states. It would rain for about four months straight; the sky was always grey, no clouds, just grey. The rain alternated between a drizzle, a downpour, and everything in between. The humidity in Vietnam was so high that during the monsoon season when the temperature would get down to 60 degrees at night, you could see your breath, just like winter in Minnesota.

We were told the choppers would be out as soon as they could fly and that we should take shelter. We were in a fairly flat landscape at the time and no real place to take cover. The winds started to pick up, and then they dramatically increased in velocity. I thought, contrary to Minnesota's tornado common sense, we should find a tree on high ground and wait for the choppers.

The weather turned really severe and a full-fledged typhoon came ashore. We stayed at the base of the tree, and when the winds became really intense, we locked arms, lying in prone positions, around the tree, and waited out the worst of it. Overall, the typhoon lasted three days, although only the afternoon of the second day did this really become overbearing. When the storm was over, the choppers were up; although when they found us there, was no dry land to set the chopper down. The lowlands were completely flooded. The best they could do was drop rubber rafts to us and had us paddle to where we could be rescued.

CO CO BEACH

The company was told we were going to have a two day stand down at Co Co Beach. Co Co Beach is an island off the mainland. This meant one thing; we would be free from any attacks and would actually be able to relax.

We learned at Co Co Beach that some of the other units would go out for one day and then have a day off. You sure could not get very far into enemy territory on a one day mission. We were called into formation as the general was coming to congratulate the O-Deuce for the distinction in earning the Vietnamese Cross of Gallantry. The colonel in charge of the visit asked if there was anyone in the formation that did not have their CIB (Combat Infantrymen's Badge), which is awarded to anyone that is in an actual combat role in a war zone. A few hands went up. He told his lieutenants to pin CIBs on everyone with their hand up and take down their name so the paperwork could be processed. He then told us that when the general asked if any one did not have a CIB to raise his hand, he did not want to see a single hand go up. This must have been his job. None of us received our paperwork.

The two days were like a dream. The ocean was beautiful, a lot of swimming; good food, well, at least, it was hot; and plenty of Coke and beer. I learned that you cannot wash shampoo out of your hair with the ocean's salt water. We had a steak fry one night; however, the steaks were dehydrated. The cooks soaked them in water for a half hour to reconstitute them, and then threw them on the grill. When the server put a steak on my plate, I looked at it and said, "Don't you guys know you are supposed to remove the veins?"

We were sitting around one night just talking and the medic said he could not believe all of the jaundice he had been seeing. He said he was treating just about every new born he came across for jaundice. I said, "They are Asian, maybe that's just the color they are when they are born." He never said anything, but he stopped treating the newborns for jaundice. I had been in country 169 days by this time and had been in the field for 154.

After Co Co Beach, we went back to the A Shau Valley for more joint operations with the 1st Cavalry and some ARVN units. The O-Deuce choppered into the A Shau Valley. Charlie Company was deployed down the center of the valley in a surprise maneuver. This was the second time Bravo Company was replaced by Charlie Company, and, again, it was a disaster. However, this time, it was from friendly fire. First, the South Vietnamese artillery was responsible for some twenty-nine casualties and fatalities. The majority of the deaths, however, were from a misguided US airstrike which killed seventy troopers. 160 went in, and fifty-one came out. We continued to run short reconnaissance missions up the Valley until we married up with the 1st Calvary to complete the operation. There were daily and frequent skirmishes with the NVA during our stints in the Valley as we conducted our hammer and anvil tactic.

LRRP

General Westmoreland was replaced by General Abrams. Along with this change came a change in how the 101st would conduct its war campaign. The enemy had learned that it could not defeat the Americans in an all out engagement, so they changed their tactics to one of small scales of numerous and frequent attacks on troops, installations, and supply lines. The NVA had adapted the tactics that had been so effective for the VC. To meet this new theater of operation, Westmorland and Abrams requested 225,000 more troops as a lot more ground would have to be covered to find increasingly smaller and smaller pockets of the enemy. President Johnson considered the proposal for two months; fearful of the public reaction, and afraid that the funding for the troops would come from his *Great Society Program*, he authorized an additional 26,000 troops. It should be kept in mind that for every one infantryman in the field, there were ten support people in other roles. Equipment and supplies have to be procured, then transported. There is also logistics, maintenance, support, medical, food, pilots, artillery, communications, and a host of other supporting roles. If we have a troop strength of 400,000, of those, 40,000 are in actual combat roles.

On 28th of June 1968, the US Army Pacific published General Order 325, which initiated reorganization of the 101st Airborne Division into the army's second airmobile division. This same order called for the Division to be redesignated the 101st Air Cavalry Division effective 1st of July 1968. The redesignation of the 101st was in line with the extensive use of helicopters in battle and the lack of any opportunity for troopers to be deployed as paratroopers and jumping into action.

The concept of paratroopers was introduced in World War II as a new means of gaining a tactical advantage over the enemy just as helicopters were introduced in Vietnam. There had been limited use of helicopters in Korea; however, they were primarily modified civilian craft and used for evacuating dead and wounded soldiers.

The French had made a parachute jump in 1954 with disastrous results. Most of their paratroopers were killed as they descended to the ground. Through some miscalculation, they had actually parachuted into two NVA training camps.

With our new commander, our tactics changed as well. We would set out in company formation to a predetermined location. Once at this location, the company would be broken up into LRRPs (Long Range Reconnaissance Patrols) and deploy for three to five day missions. Our missions were primarily to locate the enemy, engage them if feasible, call in artillery or airstrikes on their position, or just gather field intelligence. We would also conduct night ambushes. These sometimes became a concern because of our small size of ten to twelve troopers. We also would search for and destroy enemy supplies, rice and munitions.

At the end of the mission, we would marry up with the rest of the company, have a hot meal, and be resupplied. The following day, we would move to a new location and repeat the three to five day LRRP activities. We would typically go out for thirty days then have a two-day break at LZ Sally or An Lo and then redeploy.

Without the resources of additional troops that Westmoreland had requested, we were often spread way too thin. The new strategy, however, of "send them out, and if they get into trouble, chopper in what help they need" worked for the most part, but I think it cost too many American lives. Often, it took too long for the reinforcements to arrive or to have choppers available. The firefights usually did not last long unless there were a substantial number of troops involved.

SEABEES

We started taking our breaks at LZ Sally because the Seabees were rebuilding the bridge at An Lo. On our last stand down at An Lo, a sergeant that had been in the Army a long time had a few drinks and went to sleep. The only time we saw alcohol on stand down was if a trooper brought a bottle of whisky back from R&R (rest and recuperation). The sergeant was woken up for his post at guard duty in the LP. During his watch, he saw one of our other LPs through a starlight scope (specially designed optics that enable night vision) and thought it was the enemy. It wasn't, it was our LP. He threw a grenade at the LP, one trooper was killed and the other two were severely wounded.

When you are in the bush, you have to be constantly at your best. Even on our breaks, we still would have to pull guard duty and be on guard for attacks. It is very unfortunate that Hollywood chooses to portray infantry soldiers in Vietnam as getting spaced out on drugs during their breaks. As far as the 101st in I Corps is concerned, these depictions are totally untrue and a gross misrepresentation of the brave soldiers that fought in that war. But it all plays into the distorted perception liberals have and want everyone to have of war because they do not have the courage to take a stand for freedom, justice, and liberty, themselves.

John Stuart Mill summed it up best when he said,

> "War is an ugly thing, but not the ugliest of things. The decayed and degraded state of moral and patriotic feeling which thinks that nothing is worth war is much worse. When a people are used as mere human instruments for firing cannon or thrusting bayonets, in the service and for selfish purposes of a master, such war degrades a people. A war to protect other human beings against tyrannical injustice; a war to give victory to their own ideas of right and good, and which is their own war, carried on for an honest purpose by their free choice,—is often the means of their regeneration. A man who has nothing for which he is willing to fight for, nothing which he cares more about than he does about his personal safety, is a miserable creature and has no chance of being free, unless made and kept so by the exertions of better men than himself."

> —John Stuart Mill,
> The Contest in America, Dissertations and
> Discussions, vol. 1, p. 26. First published in
> Frasers Magazine, February 1862.

The anti-war protest of the Vietnam War were staged by those unwilling to fight for the freedom of an oppressed people and unwilling to defend the ideals that America stands for. In actuality, they were protesting the draft under the guise of an immoral war. They were simply afraid of going to war.

We have been involved in the war in the Middle East for thirteen years, much longer than Vietnam, yet there are no protests. The sole reason for the lack of protests, today, is that we have an all-volunteer Army, those lacking the courage to fight will not be asked to fight, so there is no reason to protest. These were not protests against the war; they were cowards protesting the draft, supported by a cowardly, and deceitful progressive news media with their own agenda.

At our next break at LZ Sally, the company clerk came up to me and said, "Lucky, you have earned your Air Medal."

I said, "What's that?"

He told me that once you have completed thirty-six chopper insertions into hot LZs, you are awarded and Air Medal.

I didn't know that, but from then on I kept track. I tried to keep track of a lot of things but with the monsoons, river crossings, and other priorities in a firefight, my journals and photos just kept getting destroyed. It was only recently when members of my family started passing away that my letters were returned to me. They had kept every one of them. The letters were very helpful in reconstructing these events and the time line.

The Seabees who were doing the construction on the bridge would receive our daily rations of Coke and beer with their normal supplies. Each trooper on the line was supposed to have a Coke and a 3.2 beer every day as part of a daily ration. We would anticipate a lot of beverages when we got back after thirty days in the field.

The Seabees, however, chose to sell our Coke rations to the Vietnamese for $20 per case so the Vietnamese children could sell us Cokes in the field for $1.00 per can. We use to wonder where they got the Cokes.

One night, while we were on a stand down at LZ Sally, our CO received a call from the commander at the bridge. He said they were under attack and fearful of being overrun. Our CO told him we would like to help but we were *just too thirsty*. Of course, we immediately saddled up into trucks and headed for An Lo, which was only a couple of miles away.

As we approached the firefight was raging, and the enemy was making a siege to our immediate left. The CO commanded "fix bayonets." We disembarked and went straight into the onslaught. This was our first hand-to-hand fighting and it was very intense.

In hand-to-hand fighting, especially at night, you have to keep advancing into the enemy because if you stop, fellow troopers will get ahead of you and into your line of fire. In hand-to-hand fighting, you shoot as long as it's safe. If you empty your magazine, there is often no time to reload, so you have to use the butt of your rifle or your bayonet. There are no fist fights in hand-to-hand combat. If you are in that situation, you use your thumb. There is no time for a fight. You stab your thumb into your opponent's eye socket, and as our drill instructor used to say, "Push until you feel goo." (Kind of makes you think about airport security, I suppose the next big idea for the TSA will be to cut off our thumbs.)

Towards the end of this engagement I found myself facing five enemy soldiers, one was at my 10:00, one at 11:00 and three more at 1:00, 2:00 and the 3:00 position. I have no memory, no recollection of how I was extracted from this excessively perilous situation.

Hand-to-hand combat is incredibly intense, it seems like you get a double shot of adrenalin. It may have had a lot to do with it being so dark and so much going on all at once. I know I have never been so busy in my whole life. We were able to beat back the attack and were never in want of our rations of Coke or beer again.

FAIL

We were again conducting operations in the villages around Hue. We were working less and less with the 1st Cavalry now as the newly designated 101st Air Cavalry began to acquire its own helicopters. One of the downsides to the redesignation of the 101st was that troopers no longer had to be qualified as paratroopers. Paratroopers are a little different breed of a warrior, and that requirement should remain in place. During World War II, prisoners of war who were paratroopers were separated from the rest of the prisoners and had twice as many guards to watch over them.

A frequent strategy employed by the VC was a staged firefight. On one occasion as we were moving parallel to a village that was supposed to be deserted. We received small arms fire from a sizable force, which forced us to take a defensive field position. The CO called for support, which was not available, so we began a squad by squad advancement towards the enemy. In a squad by squad advancement, several fire teams will lay down suppressing fire while another fire team advances. This procedure is repeated until we have a majority of our force engaging the enemy position. We would leave a couple of fire teams back as Charlie frequently would attack from the rear. Then suddenly, the firing from the village would stop.

Typically, we would form a line and sweep through the village. The villages were surrounded by bamboo hedgerows, which were very thick. They provided excellent cover for tunnel entrances and concealing booby traps.

In this instance, when I came through the hedgerow, I was facing a pink stucco two-story single family dwelling, which was very rare for anywhere in Vietnam. I stopped briefly to make sure there wasn't anyone in the house. There was a sidewalk of sorts paralleling the side of the house with a hedge on the opposite side of the sidewalk that ran down to a path that paralleled a river. I walked down the sidewalk and there was another trooper on the other side of the hedge, but because I had stopped to check the house, he was ahead of me. He reached the end of the path before I did, and just as he was approaching the end, he tripped a booby trap and was severely wounded. I ran to his aid and immediately tried to stop the bleeding. I yelled for the medic. I remember thinking, if I can just stop the blood from coming out, he will be okay. When the medic arrived, he said, "There is too much blood, I can't see anything, I need some water!"

I told one of the troopers that had gathered to grab some helmets and go back up the sidewalk I had just come down, and that there was a rain barrel at the corner of the pink house. Someone said the river is closer, and the medic said the river water was too dirty. He grabbed three or four helmets and started up the sidewalk I had just come down. He got about half way to the house and tripped a booby trap. The booby trap took both of his legs.

It is inexplicable how I did not set off the booby trap when I first came down the sidewalk. We lost both of the troopers; their wounds were just too extensive. I have never felt so useless and absolutely helpless as when I tried to save that trooper's life and failed.

There was no sign of Charlie; once they lure you into the area they have laden with booby traps, they disperse and disappear into underground tunnels. After the medivacs left, we joined up with the rest of the company.

MORAL FIBER

When we would set up a perimeter for the night, we would send out several small reconnaissance teams to make sure the immediate area was secured. The recon teams would walk a clover leaf pattern and return to the perimeter at the end of the patrol. On one of these occasions, a platoon sergeant, myself, and two privates were scouting. We came to a break in the terrain, and when a Vietnamese saw us, he began running. We fired a couple of shots and wounded him. He turned around and surrendered.

I was on guard, and the sergeant, who was my superior, searched our prisoner. He found eight hundred dollars in cash on him. He declared, "We have a North Vietnamese tax collector. We'll dust him and split the money, two hundred dollars per head."

Just to put this in perspective: Our pay, well, mine anyway, was $240 per month. In that $240 was $55 per month for being a paratrooper and $50 per month for hazardous duty pay for being in a war zone. I told the Sergeant, "We were not going to murder someone for money."

He replied, "He is an enemy combatant, and we were in a combat zone, so it wouldn't be murder."

I said, "That all changed when he surrendered."

The Sergeant pulled out his .45 pistol and put it to the prisoners head. Then he heard the safety on my M16 go off. He looked at me and my M16 was pointed right at him. I repeated, "We are not going to commit murder."

He holstered his weapon and went on a rant about how I would not survive the next firefight, "You're a dead man."

The tax collectors were from the north, and they would work with the VC to extort money from the local population to support the war effort. The next time we were involved in a firefight, I heard that the sergeant had been wounded by shrapnel and would be going back to the states for treatment.

After I finished my tour of duty in Vietnam, I was stationed at Fort Bragg, North Carolina, where most of the returning paratroopers were sent. We were sent to Fort Bragg because this was the home of the 82nd Airborne Division, and we could continue our parachuting to remain qualified as paratroopers.

I made an additional thirty-four jumps while I was at Fort Bragg. To maintain your airborne status, you had to make a parachute jump every ninety days. Although, I was only at Ft Bragg for eighteen months before I was honorably discharged, many troopers had lost their affinity for jumping. I took the opportunity to jump in their place. I always enjoyed parachuting. I ran into this sergeant at Fort Bragg, and when he saw that I recognized him, he was not able to even look at me.

I often wonder how different our lives would have turned out had he murdered our prisoner.

Sometimes, people cannot talk about their war experience because they are ashamed of things they have done.

It's all about moral fiber. Moral fiber is not some thing you are born with, it is a combination of what you learn and who you are—your character. When I say *what you learn*, that means that at any given point in time, we are a culmination of our experiences and the information we have judged to be true. Because we judge some information to be true, we incorporate it into our personal worldview.

Reality is as reality is perceived and both experiences and things we learn change our perception of reality. What is real for me may not be real for you. I know wasps mean something to me that is completely different than what wasps mean for just about anyone else. That is the same as the meanings I hold for freedom, liberty, justice, and one nation under God. We all have a variety of experiences and a cognitive process that we used to gain information and make judgments about what we know. Some information we decide to discard and some we choose to hold as life's truths. To put a finer point on it, based on what we know, we make judgments about our values. Our values guide us as to what is appropriate behavior and what is inappropriate.

If you are the sole determining factor in your values, your interests will be self-centered and self-serving. If you are aware of the teachings of Jesus Christ, you will try to be righteous in your understanding of life, humanity, and in your behavior. Righteous simply means that you and your actions are right or aligned with God. The caveat in this whole enterprise is that if you are one of God's elect, He will not let you stray very far from His path. He has put within you His spirit, which serves as a guide for our eternal existence, not just a monitor of our brief stay on earth. The simple truth is that we are made for an eternal existence. We are made for eternity, not for the seventy or so years we are on earth. Our behavior has consequences for that eternity.

Those who do not grasp the reality of our eternal existence live for today, the "you only go around once," or "what do you have to lose?" crowd. The answer is everything. It is true you only go around once; however, that one time has eternal consequences.

The true test of your moral fiber or your courage and bravery are not as you envision it. It is how you behave when situations are real and there are real consequences for your behavior. Consequences not between you and man or you and the law, but consequences between you and God. Life matters, nothing happens by accident, and God is watching.

We continued to conduct missions for our thirty days, then the CO decided to skip our break so we stayed out for another thirty days. Several times, our LRRPs would get cut off or run into such a superior force we could not engage them. Twice during this time, our team could not marry up with the company and we went four days, on both occasions, without being resupplied with food or water. It was hard to find good water to drink, and when you did, you had to put an iodine pill into the water and wait a half hour before it was safe to drink. There were times when we had to fill our canteens from stagnant pools of water; I always had a bad sense about doing this. But you have to have water. I would break through the surface and try to get my canteen as deep into the pool as I could.

When I was discharged from the army, I had to report to Ft. Snelling to be tested for Agent Orange. After the tests, I was told that the concentration of Agent Orange in my system was so high that I should not be a blood donor. I was never in an area where actual spraying was being conducted; however, I was in areas where spraying had been done. I imagine I picked up the Agent Orange from these stagnant pools of water.

Without resupplies, the water was questionable and there was no food to be found. We learned early on that if we ate the rice we would get dysentery. When you go four days without food, the expression is "if you're hungry enough, you will eat anything." I beg to differ. Our commander wanted to provide us with a very nutritious meal when we finally got back, so they flew in liver and onions with mashed potatoes. I took one bite of the liver and traded it for someone's mashed potatoes.

The next time we went four days without food and water, we had married up with the rest of the company by a river and were told the helicopters would not be coming in because of the low ceiling. I was really hungry, and as a Minnesotan, I kept looking at the river wondering what kind of fish are there in the waters of Vietnam.

I pulled out a grenade, pulled the pin, and threw it into the river. I didn't warn anyone because I knew the water would muffle the explosion. A couple of troopers saw me toss the grenade; they looked at me, then at the river. Within seconds about fifty fish floated belly-up to the surface. We started to collect the fish and all of a sudden everyone was on board, we were going to have a fish fry. I wondered what a grenade would do in my favorite fishing hole in Minnesota.

On one of our LRRP patrols, we got into a firefight, we started with fourteen When it was over, there were six of us left. The sergeant said he would get us out of there, but the rest of the troopers said, we want Lucky to lead us out.

This sergeant had not done a lot to engender the confidence of the troops. One time as we were coming into a village, there was a very upset Water Buffalo blocking our path. We stopped trying to figure out how to best the creature. The sergeant walked up to the Water Buffalo and grabbed him by the horns. The Buffalo twisted his head to the left and to the right. The sergeant looking like a rag doll as he bounced off the path on the right and on the left. Scotty walked up, fired a burst from his M16 into the Buffalo. Of course all the villagers raised cane and we had to pay for the Water Buffalo.

The sergeant also once had a skull that he carried on a long poll sticking out of his rucksack. I think he thought it was some kind of a personal psychological operation that he would use to defeat the enemy. We got him to give up his personal agenda. I took the lead and was able to bring us back safely at our rendez-vous point.

On one of our breaks at LZ Sally, the company clerk asked me to stop by and see him when I had some time. Our third CO was not liked or respected by the men, he took too many unnecessary chances, and then to our dismay, he extended his tour on line for another two months.

When I came in to see the company clerk, he had left the medical records for our CO open and lying on the table. We talked briefly, and then he excused him-self. I looked down at the records and the page it was open to and read that one of our COs parents had com-mitted suicide. A few months later, the other one fol-lowed suit. It then said our CO was under psychiatric care for eighteen months.

A lot of things started running through my mind. Is this why he seems to be so reckless with regard for the safety of the troops? Does he think he has something to prove? The life of one trooper is not worth the career of one captain or any officer for that matter. Unless they choose to make that sacrifice. The information troubled me, but I could see no good coming from telling any-one. That kind of information would only demoralize everyone. Some things are just better left unsaid.

INTERVENTION

The Seabee's finished with their construction of the An Lo Bridge. We resumed taking our stand downs at the bridge. We were leaving An Lo for a thirty-day LRRP mission, so we were at company strength. We came to a river that we would have to cross. There is a tendency for a line of troops to get bunched up before a crossing, and that is just when the ambush started. I was already in the river so I headed for the nearest river bank only to discover that everyone was pinned down.

One machine gun was firing at the head of the formation where everyone was backed up. The other machine gun was firing at the back, working towards the middle. I looked up to the top of the bank where one of my friends was shouting orders, only to see him get shot in the head. Troopers were dying.

I removed the LAW from my rucksack and fired it at the enemy position; it was a direct hit and took out both of the machine guns.

I was recommended for a Silver Star; however, it was denied as I had violated the terms of the Geneva

Convention. You cannot use a LAW against troops, unless they are in an armored vehicle.

The CO said that this was bull—t, he said he would figure out a way to at least have an Army Commendation awarded for taking out the machine gun nest. However, the Commendation could not be associated with the LAW incident.

The several Geneva Conventions are an attempt to add rules and guidelines for war. Soldiers from God-fearing countries do not really need them and usually conduct themselves with honor, granted a few sociopaths do slip through and into the system at times. The rules, for the most part, are for soldier of godless nations who do not answer to a higher power and fear no repercussions for their actions. Those who need the guidelines most are the ones who give the least amount of credence to the guidelines.

We rounded the hedgerow from where the ambush had occurred, only to find a plot of trees, one hundred meters by three hundred meters. We surmised the remainder of the force would be in the woods. We swept through the woods and found no one. The only conclusion was there must be tunnels under the woods.

The CO moved all of the troopers back and called in an airstrike. He positioned the three-point men around the perimeter of the woods; my post was on the long axis of the woods. The two F-4s came in and dropped their payload, only to have one of the five hundred–pound bombs bounce out of the woods and tumble end over end directly to where I was standing. I knew it would be fruitless to try and run in the mud of the rice patties, besides, I would never have gotten far enough away. I just watched the bomb tumbling through the air to where I was standing. As I looked at the unexploded bomb that landed fifteen feet in front of me, I said, "Okay, I get this! This has nothing to do with me. You are in charge, and it is all according to Your will."

This was September eighteenth. It was then I realized between the several narrow escapes, twenty-six to be exact, that I was aware of, the out of body experience, and, now, the bomb, that I was not in control of any of the events that were transpiring. This and all of the other events were in God's hand, my fate lied in God's hands alone. My safety had nothing to do with my military experience, training, or personal ability. I read somewhere that: "Safety is not in the absence of danger, but in the presence of the LORD."

I surmised from all of my experiences that I was bullet proof until the day God called me home. That is a very dangerous thing to say, because I would not want anyone to assume that it applies to them as well. We do not know the plans that God has for us and they are different for each one of us. When I realized that I was bullet proof, I became less cautious—not careless, just less cautious.

After the airstrike, we walked through the wooded area. We found the tunnel entrances and the area was the home of an underground hospital with 148 beds. There were nineteen dead, and we had taken nineteen prisoners. We do not know how many were trapped in what remained of the hospital.

I was looking at one of the prisoners. He was covered in soot from the napalm, and he was terrified. I offered him my canteen and a cigarette, for which he was very appreciative. I think it just let him know that we meant no further harm.

The hospital had a concrete ceiling. That is why the bomb glanced off and out of the woods, and it did not detonate because—I wonder how *ministering spirits* disarm bombs that are in flight.

We continued operations in the villages around Hue as well as in the A Shau Valley for the next couple of months. The Valley was essentially several valleys and mountains. As a major entry point to South Vietnam from the Ho Chi Minh trail, it was critical to the North Vietnamese as their conduit for supplies, additional troops, and communications for units of the NVA and VC operating in I Corps. Because of its significance to the NVA and VC, it was the target of continual major operations by allied forces, especially the 101st Air Cavalry. Also, it was defended vehemently by the NVA and VC. There were no outposts in the Valley; after Khe Sanh they had all been abandoned. The O-Deuce would be sent in whenever the intelligence community reported a high concentration of enemy activity. The Valley was the scene of a great deal of fighting throughout the war, and it acquired a fearsome reputation for soldiers on both sides. Being a veteran of t*he Valley*, became a mark of distinction among combat veterans.

The most famous battle in the Valley was Operation Apache Snow, also known as Hamburger Hill, conducted by the 101st and ARVN units where seventy-two troopers were killed and 630 NVA. The second most dangerous job in Vietnam was to be an infantryman for the US; the most dangerous job was to be an infantryman for the communists.

I still had not had my R & R. We were supposed to have a five-day-in-country R & R after three months in the field. In-country R & Rs were in III Corps, in areas that were well secured. After six months, we were supposed to have a seven-day R & R out of country, in places like Sydney, Bangkok, Tokyo, or Hawaii.

In November, it was time for our current CO to rotate back to the states. Our fourth CO arrived at An Lo Bridge while we were on a two-day stand down. The new CO asked to see me. The conversation went something like this:

"Newman, by looking at your records, it appears that you have not had your in-country R & R, is that right?

"That is correct, Sir."

"It also appears that you have not had an out-of-country R & R is that right?"

"That is also correct, Sir."

"So you have been in the field for 250 days without a break?"

"That is correct, Sir"

"Trooper, you have done enough, and more than most. Where do you want to go for R & R?"

"I would like to go to Hawaii for Christmas."

"Lieutenant, make that happen! I am not sending you back into the field. You can report to LZ Sally upon your return from R & R and train new recruits on the tactics of the VC and the NVA and prepare them for what's ahead."

"Thank you, Sir."

It was over.

EPILOGUE

When I first returned from Vietnam, I had a lot of things to figure out, a lot of questions. I had to contend with survivor's guilt from 97 percent casualties and fatalities; why them and not me? There was also the twenty-six times I should have been killed or at least severely wounded and wasn't, like the path by the rain barrel. And what about the wasps? Living in a different dimension without a physical body? There was also the anger for the way we were treated on our return home. This was compounded with the deceitful and biased news reporting that was being perpetuated by the media. It appeared most folks bought into the lies of the cowards of protest and the corroborate guile of the media. The news and protesters had regulated us to *baby burners* while the unspoken personal stories were ones of honor, bravery, and personal sacrifice.

When I arrived stateside into Connecticut, I was told at the airport to go to the USO Lounge and not to be in the terminal until my flight departure was announced. US Military uniforms were not welcomed in the airport.

These were the same people so many had died for—for freedom, for liberty, for the values of the United States of America.

"It is foolish and wrong to mourn the men who died. Rather, we should thank God that such men lived," said Gen. George Patton.

When I returned to Minnesota, I attended the University of Minnesota looking for answers to all my questions. The answers were not at the University. The information they taught is strictly about this reality and all with a distinctive liberal bias, which severely limits the scope of inquiry.

I tried to put it all behind me. I became involved in a career and got married. Then the miracle of birth brought all of those unanswered questions back to the forefront.

I had looked for answers everywhere, except in Scripture, so I began there. After the birth of my children, I started getting up at 5:00 a.m. to spend an hour in Scripture before I began my daily routine.

There is a lot in information in Scripture about foundational reality. I found the answers to the why questions that had been lingering since 1968; questions about life, death, faith, and eternity. Questions about how a God of love could allow war to happen and questions about life in another dimension.

The answers to those questions I published in *A Brief History of the Bible: The Essentials of Christianity within the Context of Our Physical and Spiritual Realities*. I suggest anyone should read *A Brief History of the Bible* if you are interested in a look at life, faith, and Scripture from someone who has been on the other side, someone who has slipped behind the veil. And to those that know they should read the Bible, but either just don't seem to have the time, or find Scripture difficult to understand.

People go through experiences and hopefully, we learn from those experiences and can pass those learning's onto others. Often, the experiences involve a fair amount of anguish and we pass along our learning's in the hope of sparing others from going through the same pain that we experienced.

If you have had some exceptionally challenging experiences, share your experience, do not waste the learning. It's kind of like if I hit someone over the head with a two by four, and this guy says to his friend, "Wow! that really hurt!" Now his friend has two choices he can take him at his word or he can say, "Well, I believe you, but I just have to find out for myself."

There was one trooper that spent all of his time in the rear at LZ Sally. He had been on a search and destroy mission and had accidentally shot and killed two troopers. He probably reacted too quickly, and the two troopers were where they should not have been. There was no good reason to make him stay in Vietnam to serve out his full tour; he needed help, which was not provided at LZ Sally.

The mindset of the military is *buck up and keep on keeping on*. This training usually results in a denial of one's issues or self-medicating with drugs and/or alcohol. These horrendous experiences we go through, and not just in war, cause scars on our souls. In our self-assumed superiority, and the denial of the reality of a sovereign God, we think we know how to treat scarred souls. All we do, however, because we *lean on our own understanding*, (Proverbs 3:5 NASB) is administer treatment to the physical manifestations of a scarred soul. We *suppress the truth* (Romans 1:18 NASB) of the power of Christ.

Scripture tells us we are *a new creation in Christ* (2 Corinthians 5:17 NASB). In that new creation is the care and treatment for a scarred soul. The act of honoring the dictates of our conscience is a freewill act, as is the decision to ignore our conscience, because we love the *things of the world* (1 John 2:15 NASB).

There is a pervasive victim mentality in our culture; someone or something is always to blame. This victim mentality means we never take responsibility for our own actions. Without taking responsibility for our actions, there is no repentance; without repentance, there is no redemption. Without redemption, the scars never go away.

When the disciple *Doubting Thomas* saw the resurrected Christ, he said, "My LORD and MY God" (John 20:28, NASB). He was the first of the disciples to get it right—Christ was God. The incarnate God came to earth. Christ was railroaded through a mock trial, ridiculed, humiliated, harassed, spit upon, tortured, flogged beyond recognition and brutally murdered. He said of His slayers, "Father, forgive them, for they do not know what they are doing" (Luke 23:34 NASB).

If you put your trust in Christ, there is no sin you have committed that cannot be forgiven.

The proof is that Christ was raised from the dead. Only God can determine what justice is demanded for sin, because all sin is an affront to God's holiness. "The wages of sin is death" (Romans 6:23 NASB) and "there is not one who is without sin" (Romans 3:12 NASB). The incarnate Christ came to earth to save us from the wrath of God. God came to save us from God that is why it all works. That could be the only propitiation, the only appeasement for God's wrath, which rests on all of us because of our sinful nature. *We are not sinners because we sin; we sin because we are sinners.* When Christ took all of our sins on Himself, He died. *The wages of sin is death* (Romans 6:23 NASB). His death paid the price for all of our sins (Colossians 1:14 NASB). With the penalty of sin paid, all sins were forgiven, and He was raised from death to life, just as we are.

The spectrum of light rays runs from gamma rays to ultraviolet rays. The human eye can only see about 10 percent of the entire light spectrum. That is the part that is provisional reality. It is the touch and feel three-dimensional reality we live in. It is physical, it is material, and it is corporal. It is predictable and governed by the physical laws of God. Our minds are able to process the information we receive from our senses and put it into some type of a context that makes sense and serves to define our reality.

Foundational reality is a completely different reality, as it exists beyond the sensitivity of our sensory receptors. Our sense of sight does not have the ability to penetrate beyond the thin veil that separates our physical reality or provisional reality from foundational reality or the spiritual realm. Foundational reality is made up of the other 90 percent of the light spectrum; it is non-corporal, non-material, it is not composed of hard matter. It is the realm of God, His celestial beings, Satan and his minions. It is the reality of a different dimension. Because of our inability to perceive attributes of foundational reality, we have a disconnection between the two realities and we have difficulty understanding their interconnectedness.

So if we are looking for answers to the real questions of life, questions about what is life, death, faith, eternity, and other dimensions, and we restrict our inquires to only that which we can see and feel in provisional reality, we exclude our ability to understand the connection with foundational reality. This means we are not considering complete or true reality. This not only limits our ability to understand supernatural intersections, it also limits our ability to find the real answers to the questions we have about the meaning and significance of our existence because we are only looking at half of the picture. We see a glimpse of foundational and provisional reality in the twenty-second chapter of the book of Numbers.

> But God was angry because he was going, and the angel of the LORD took his stand in the way as an adversary against him. Now he was riding on his donkey and his two servants were with him. When the donkey saw the angel of the LORD standing in the way with his drawn sword in his hand, the donkey turned off from the way and went into the field; but Balaam

struck the donkey to turn her back into the way.
Then the angel of the LORD stood in a narrow
path of the vineyards, with a wall on this side
and a wall on that side. When the donkey saw
the angel of the LORD, she pressed herself to the
wall and pressed Balaam's foot against the wall,
so he struck her again. The angel of the LORD
went further, and stood in a narrow place where
there was no way to turn to the right hand or
the left. When the donkey saw the angel of the
LORD, she lay down under Balaam; so Balaam
was angry and struck the donkey with his stick.
And the LORD opened the mouth of the donkey,
and she said to Balaam, "What have I done to
you, that you have struck me these three times?"
Then Balaam said to the donkey, "Because you
have made a mockery of me! If there had been
a sword in my hand, I would have killed you by
now." The donkey said to Balaam, "Am I not
your donkey on which you have ridden all your
life to this day? Have I ever been accustomed
to do so to you?" And he said, "No." Then the
LORD opened the eyes of Balaam, and he saw
the angel of the LORD standing in the way with
his drawn sword in his hand; and he bowed all
the way to the ground. The angel of the LORD
said to him, "Why have you struck your donkey
these three times? Behold, I have come out as
an adversary, because your way was contrary to
me. But the donkey saw me and turned aside
from me these three times. If she had not turned
aside from me, I would surely have killed you
just now, and let her live." Balaam said to the
angel of the LORD, "I have sinned, for I did not

know that you were standing in the way against me. Now then, if it is displeasing to you, I will turn back." But the angel of the Lord said to Balaam, "Go with the men, but you shall speak only the word which I tell you." So Balaam went along with the leaders of Balak.

Numbers 22:22–35 (NASB)

There are consequences for limiting our understanding to just provisional reality. We suppress the truth of the Gospel and we trade it for a lie, we are *self-deceived*. Scripture tells us that we "Traded the truth for the lie" (Rom 1:25 NASB) because "men loved the darkness rather than the light" (John 3:19 NASB). When we limit our understanding to just provisional reality, we come up with things like the theory of evolution.

God had to be discredited; creation (the truth) had to be replaced with the theory of evolution (the lie). Then we are not accountable to a higher authority and may do as we please. It's a lie because it is contrary to the truth. God as the Creator of all things is the only one that can define truth, it is His reality. Everyone intuitively understands this, but some refuse to acknowledge this truth that is why God calls it suppressing the truth.

The theory of evolution is the same mindset that held that the earth was flat. When Darwin was hatching this theory, science was just beginning to develop cell theory. They didn't have a clue about DNA. This was the same year Louis Pasteur said, "Hey, dummies, life just doesn't mysteriously happen, flies lay eggs, and when they hatch we get maggots." And all the people said, "Oh." When people used to see maggots just appear on meat, they thought, *Life just happens.* They didn't know that flies laid eggs.

The theory of evolution states that life just happened from organic matter, and that over time, things in provisional reality just evolved, continued to develop. Evolution attempts to explain the brain, but cannot explain the mind or consciousness. Evolution attempts to explain the body but cannot explain the spirit or the soul. Evolution cannot explain anything in foundational reality. Darwin even said that if the fossil record did not support his theory, then he was wrong. There was not much fossil evidence at the time. However, we have a lot of fossils evidence now, and nothing supports his theory. There are no—notta, zero—fossils that show a transitional phase of a species changing from one species into another.

So why do we hold onto the lies, like the theory of evolution, and teach them to our kids in school? Because the progressive agenda is to suppress the truth. "We don't want this man to rule over us"(Luke 19:14 NASB). And "men loved the darkness rather than the light, because their deeds were evil" (John 3:19 NASB). And why do we suppress the truth? (Romans 1:18 NASB). "The pride of life, and the lust of the flesh" (1 John 2:16 NASB). By suppressing the truth and promoting the lie, the attempt is made to discredit God, so that He is no longer relevant. If God is no longer relevant to Americans, then the Constitution and our inalienable rights can be rendered null and void.

Our Founding Fathers, after witnessing the Providence of God in the founding of our Nation and the miracles of the Revolutionary War, understood as Ben Franklin pointed out, "God governs in the affairs of men." They also understood that man was account-able to God for his actions and inactions. However, if God can be discredited, man can do as he pleases; there is no accountability.

How will we answer the question of what is right and what is wrong? Will we go back to the Law of Moses, or manmade laws? The only rights we will be left with are the ones prescribed by man, and any right given by a man can be taken away by a man.

Our founding documents are based on the Word and law of God because our Founders understood man was a fallen creature and could not be his own lawgiver and judge as it is explained in the book of Deuteronomy.

God as the creator of all things is the only one that can define truth; it is His reality.

George Washington said, "Of all the dispositions and habits which lead to political prosperity, religion and morality are indispensable supports. In vain would that man claim the tribute of patriotism, who should labor to subvert these great pillars of human happiness…"

The two pillars George Washington talked about; morality and religion are integral to a strong America. Something miraculous needs to happen in the heart and soul of America.

My experience in the MASH unit in Vietnam had a profound impact on my interpretation of Scripture. When we read Scripture, we tend to pass much of it off as metaphorical. However, real significance and meaning for this life is contingent upon understanding the connection between these two realities.

We will only be in this reality for seventy years, give or take some. But foundational reality is forever.

There are two layers of meaning, in just about everything, provisional and foundational. Scripture falls into the dual-meaning category, especially the parables of Christ. His parables are spoken in the language of provisional reality; however, their meaning and significance can only be seen from a perspective of foundational reality.

When I flat-lined, I left provisional reality, my body stayed behind because that was its reality. My spirit, which is the life force from God within us, and my soul, which is who we are as individuals, went into foundational reality because that is their realm. We are not made for provisional reality; we are made for eternity—for foundational reality.

In the operating room, I could see all that was transpiring in provisional reality. However, they were not able to see me, nor were they even aware that I was in the room. I had slipped behind the veil. We do not acknowledge the interconnectedness of the two realities.

Reality is as reality is perceived, and we behave according to our perception of reality. When you acknowledge the existence of both realities and that, in a sense, we live right now in both of them, as we are both physical and spiritual beings; this acknowledgement becomes our new reality with corresponding new behaviors.

Everyone that I know that is a Christian, we will know each other for all of eternity. For me that has a profound impact on my relationships because our relationships are the only thing we will take with us from provisional reality into foundation reality.

All of Christ's disciples had a hard time leaving their beliefs of provisional reality behind. They could not quite grasp what Christ was talking about when He talked about the kingdom, and especially about it being at hand.

During Christ's trial, all the disciples were cowards, Peter denied Christ three times, someone ran out of the Garden of Gethsemane naked to avoid capture. They hid in a room with the doors locked.

They never really understood until they saw the risen Christ. Then they were empowered to preach and give their lives as martyrs for the faith. What changed? They saw Christ in His resurrected state; they now knew life after death was a reality. Christians believe that as a Christian, they will have eternal life, but like the disciples, they did not know it, they only believed it.

I know life after death is real, I get it. I don't believe it, I know it. Get what? True faith, that's the faith Abraham had when he was willing to sacrifice Isaac on the altar. When God stopped him, He said, "Do not stretch out your hand against the lad, and do nothing to him; for now I know that you fear God, since you have not withheld your son, your only son, from Me" (Genesis 22:12 NASB). That's all in."

The spiritual gift of prophecy is not restricted in its meaning to the foretelling of future events. It also entails the concept of revelation from the Holy Spirit of God's Word based on unique personal experiences that God has orchestrated in our lives.

> For we do not want you to be unaware, brethren, of our affliction which came to us in Asia, that we were burdened excessively, beyond our strength, so that we despaired even of life; indeed, we had the sentence of death within ourselves so that we would not trust in ourselves, but in God who raises the dead; who delivered us from so great a peril of death, and will deliver us, He on whom we have set our hope. And He will yet deliver us, you also joining in helping us through your prayers, so that thanks may be given by many persons on our behalf for the favor bestowed on us through the prayers of many.
>
> 2 Corinthians 1:8–11 (NASB)

ABOUT THE AUTHOR

Tom Newman is also the author of *A Brief History of the Bible: The Essentials of Christianity within the Context of Our Physical and Spiritual Realities.*

"God has given Tom Newman a wonderful revelation into the truth of Jesus Christ as Lord and Savior. This is simply one of the best books I've ever read that gives great insight into Biblical truth and prophecy. This book delivers on spirit-led vision and truth of what God means about the past, present, and future. Essentially, it's an accurate and condensed version of the Bible. The interpretation of what was, what is, and what is to come on earth, in about 20% of the Bible's length, is right on and good news for believers. If you have not (or cannot) read the entire Bible, then I'd recommend this book as it reveals the Truth in Jesus Christ."

—John Kolstad, Superior, WI

"This book is a must read for anyone interested in biblical truth, whether a mature Christian, someone new to the faith, or you're just curious about the

Christian faith in general. The Bible can be difficult
to read study and understand. Tom has done all of the
heavy lifting for you. This book is the product of over
20 years of bible study and research. He does an excellent job of explaining the spiritual teaching contained
in scripture and helps you understand God's purpose
for His creation. I'm not much of a reader myself, but
I can honestly say that once I started *A Brief History of
the Bible*, I couldn't put it down. My own understanding
of the Bible has been greatly enhanced after reading
Tom's book."

—**Frank Reiter, Minnesota**

"I remember as a young man growing up not having any religious guidance from either parent. This of
course led to many questions that where unanswered.
At the age of 28 all my questions where answered; like a
ray of faith cutting through the fog of a hopeless abyss.
The answers came to me in the form of a book entitled:
A Brief History of the Bible. The book was recommended
to me by a close friend that could see how I was looking
for truth and understanding in a world that has made
it hard to find. I now can honestly say that I now know
what inner peace feels like, and I am forever indebted
to my friend. *A Brief History of the Bible* is a revolutionary book; of the authors real life experiences with his
own struggle with religious falsehoods and realities. He
draws you in with his personal life, and interprets the
scripture for more of a complete understanding of what
was being conveyed."

—**Jeremiah M Belisle, Savage, MN**